At Home
with Southern Living

At Home
with Southern Living

Edited by
Katherine Pearson

Introduction by Philip Morris

With the Homes Staff
of SOUTHERN LIVING® Magazine

Louis Joyner
Carole Engle
Ernest Wood
Carolyn Rhodes
Deborah Hastings
Tynette Cerniglia
Bob Lancaster
Mac Jamieson

Oxmoor
House®

At Home with Southern Living®

Editor: Karen Phillips Irons
Design: Carol Middleton
Editorial Assistants: Patty E. Howdon, Lisa Gant,
    Pamela Hall
Special Assistance, Editing: Ellen Sullivan
Art: Susan Waldrip
Production: Jerry Higdon, Jane Bonds, Jim Thomas
Special Assistance: David Morrison
Art Director: Bob Nance

Table of Contents

Introduction

There is substance to a frequently made observation that Southerners are in love with their houses. The homes tours that mark spring like opening azaleas, the attention lavished on historic houses in every town and county, the care taken with even the newest house at the end of a just-planted walk so everything will be right for family, friends, and visitors—all attest to the fond compulsion that transforms bricks and beams and newel posts into affairs of the heart.

And like so much else in the South, this emotion is shared. It's not enough to love *your* house; you have to love as many *others* as you can. That's why the tours of houses are such musical events, with choruses of comment in melodic accents about one lovely detail or another. This is a book meant to put such into print. We can't capture the voices, but the pages speak directly and expressively about what a region of house lovers admires in a house.

The *Southern Living* way with homes has reflected the philosophy of the magazine, to be helpful and believable and thorough but with a consistent sense of style. And style in the South has less to do with fashion—with this year's color or that year's look—and more to do with the interplay between long-term traditions of style and individual expression. Yes, taste does tend to be conservative, but the rules and expectations do provide a common language: Like good dinner conversation, a room in a house should be lively, not shocking. And above all else, the house should be comfortable in the roundest sense of the word. Few want anything

that might be called a "showplace." There should be a proper formal dining room, certainly, and some fine antiques (preferably from the family), and a well-proportioned entry hall (sparkling a little, but not glittering). These lead gracefully back to a large room with painted paneling (lots of plop-down-into seating here and a big low table that won't be hurt if feet wind up there). In view is the terrace and garden and a kitchen that looks a little like something from the farm except for all that equipment and the wine rack.

That's the kind of house *Southern Living* editors and photographers have spent their recent lives visiting, often spending the day and just as often sitting down to dinner with the hospitable owners. Real houses, we like to say, though we don't think that is an adequate description. Somebody always does live there, though, and they tell us all about it. By visiting each house and taking time to find out what is most attractive and helpful to pass along, we have found some truth. We recall, for example, the handsome oversize stone fireplace with a wide, wide opening, built from a photograph in a magazine. We expressed interest, but the owners said there was a small problem—it didn't draw. We turned our camera the other way, to proven features.

There have been more than enough lovely houses and workable ideas to fill weeks of sociable rambling through every state, most cities, many, many towns, and some far country places across the South. What has been selected from those countless forays and thousands of photographs to appear in this book, we think, represents the essence of *Southern Living* homes presentation and a fully realized picture of what one glimpses through glowing windows along Pineridge Avenue, Peachtree Circle, Fairoaks Lane, or any of the region's appealing residential streets. The book includes complete houses with accompanying floor plans that provide a style overview. The diversity may be surprising to some. Despite the image of the Greek Revival antebellum house that symbolizes the South in many minds, the region's residential architecture has always been diverse, and our selection expresses that.

There is great emphasis put upon adding on and remodeling with chapters about each. For good reason, Southerners have been leaders in the movement to stay put and redo. They like the location, they love their neighborhood, the chance to make a place exactly what they would like is irresistible. Many complete examples are given of additions and remodeling, along with some general points about how to design and execute either successfully. Information is also included about working with architects and interior designers. These professionals have been of great help to our editors over the years, taking time to show us their work and even helping get the final touches set for photography. Contrary to some who feel designers inhibit personal expression, we have found most do a fine job of helping people get exactly what they want. Many have become our personal friends, just as they are to clients.

Kitchens are a central focus of the book just as they are for so many houses. It seems everyone wants an inviting kitchen at least partly open, to the area where entertaining or family activity takes place. Time and again we have heard homeowners say, "Everyone winds up in the kitchen anyway, so we wanted it to be a nice place to be in." Again, there are many complete examples and some generalized tips on good kitchen organization, equipment, and other important features. Much of *Southern Living's* attention has been given to problem-solving, and this is particularly true of kitchens.

The problem with the next type of room is often what to call it. Family room? Activity room? All-purpose or greatroom? That is an indication of how many different ways this evolving space can turn. In the fullest sense this is the true living room of today, where the most people come together the most often for the most varied purposes. It tends to be large and the place for greatest personal expression, and because the living takes so many directions, often the major design issue here is to accommodate varied uses with functional wall units, zones of seating and dining, and well-defined circulation. Most family living rooms need to be at once comfortable enough for day-to-day and dressy enough for entertaining. Our examples show how this can be done.

Formality has never lost its appeal for the South, though it is freely balanced with the more informal now, and the strongholds for this reservoir of beautiful wood finishes, rich fabrics, crystal, and fine art objects remain the formal living and dining rooms. Within the total context of the house, these often serve as adult retreats. But they are also the place where heirlooms are placed to be sat upon or dined upon, of course, but with respect and care. Because they are less often used, they are more special to occasions when they are. The chapter on living and dining rooms indicates how personal these more formal elements can be even while holding the door against the too common.

The place to begin the love affair with the garden and natural environs for growing numbers of Southern homeowners and remodelers is the garden room. When we first began doing them they were often still called Florida rooms, but the concept has evolved many times over since then. Like the family living room, the garden room can be anything, and it is not uncommon to see these two rooms combined. The operating factor is light (mostly from skylights and views from generous outside walls of glass). Light attracts people, and the views let you enjoy the garden whatever the season. Such rooms also emphasize easy movement between inside and outside via French doors or other ready access, allowing them to expand into the garden as the season permits. We have even seen the return of the open-air room lately as people find ways to extend the number of days a week and weeks a year without conditioned air.

A sense of working with the environment has always been an important part of *Southern Living* homes selection. We have looked for houses that go out of their way to respect a beautiful wooded site, to orient properly for sun and breeze, to make the most of what nature has provided in the way of views and other amenities. This book's extensive chapter on this multifaceted topic stands as testimony to the regional awareness we have cultivated over the years, and elaborates on a matter of great concern for most of us as we build or remodel.

The book concludes with a chapter on personal style, the counterpole to regional style mentioned above. These are wonderful examples of just how full and original—almost eccentric—houses can be as a reflection of individual likes. These are the kinds of houses that in the South you may hear people talking about for counties around, while they figure out how to get you in to see. It is that extra measure of personality and individual expression we think comes through in these pages, the feeling of houses lived in and loved a little beyond reason.

We remember a young couple outside a small North Carolina town we visited once who had largely restored an eighteenth-century gambrel-roofed house moved from land originally owned by his family. Both were schoolteachers, but they were slowly, carefully doing everything just right, had even sent their doors away to Virginia to be redone properly. And the basement was to be their true eighteenth-century room to the last detail. Not even electricity. They hadn't completed it, and it might be the devil to photograph by candlelight, but maybe someday. . . . So this is a story without an end, and we like it that way. We hope you do, too.

Philip Morris
Executive Editor, SOUTHERN LIVING

Southern Style

It would be hard to pin-point a singular Southern style. These homes— whether contemporary or traditional—are shaped both by a sense of place (climate, site, architectural heritage) and by the active life-styles of the families they shelter. Here is a sampling of all of the traditions that together tell a story about Southern style.

Classic Stucco Revives a Coastal Tradition

This home on Sea Island, Georgia, echoes a style of architecture used here earlier. It is both friendly and as romantic as the setting.

The Regency style is no stranger to the Southern seacoast. The style was popular in Savannah and other coastal cities early in the nineteenth century. Characterized by simple, straight lines, stuccoed exterior walls, and boxy massing, the Regency style derives its name from its popularity during the Regency of George, Prince of Wales.

The architect/owner of this island home wanted more flexibility, however, than was offered by strict adherence to formal Regency styling. Classical elements of the Regency style are here—the shell motif, Oriental details, and antiques of the period. But the house has a feeling of relaxed formality more appropriate to coastal living and today's life-styles.

Lighter woods are generally associated with informality, and the architect has used heart-pine doors at the entry and elsewhere in the house to relax the setting. Neutral color schemes for all but the most formal rooms also contribute to a friendly welcome despite formal furnishings. The result is a more livable adaptation of the true Regency style, and this friendly tradition is as much a part of the Southern style now as Regency was in the nineteenth century.

Above, right: Two shades of light terra-cotta were used on the exterior stucco. To separate the colors, a darker 8-inch-wide band was brushed and allowed to set without being smoothed.

Left: The windows are tall and narrow in the Regency tradition, with wrought-iron balconies on the second story. Arched shutters with a fan-shaped top frame the front entry.

Above: A rich gold and mellow blue in the pagoda-design wallpaper establish the color scheme for the dining room.

Right: Built-in bookcases flank the fireplace. The center section of each bookcase is capped with a shell motif framed by arched heart-pine doors.

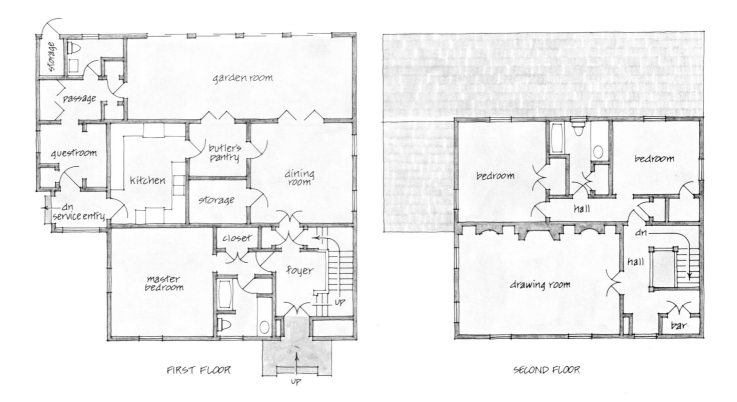

FIRST FLOOR

SECOND FLOOR

House Fits Old Neighborhood, New Life-Styles

This new house blends in with Charlotte's historic Fourth Ward with a design that reflects the best of old and new architecture. It slips into the neighborhood in a way as unique as its design: sideways.

Most people who visit this Charlotte, North Carolina, home think it is an old house that has been renovated. It is not. Despite the steeply pitched three-gable roof, bay window, and weatherboard siding that matches its Victorian neighbors, this is a new house. It was carefully designed to blend into Charlotte's historic Fourth Ward neighborhood.

This, however, is not re-created Victoriana. The house has skylights, metal chimneys, and a deck. Inside, where a solar greenhouse floods living areas with light, the home is thoroughly contemporary. The owner recalls, "We wanted a house that would be really up-to-date regarding energy and open space and sunlight."

The young family moved from the suburbs to live downtown for the convenience to theaters, museums, work, and shopping. They did not want the headaches of restoring an old house, but they did recognize the importance of blending their home into an historic neighborhood.

Their architect turned the side of the house to the street to make the most of a deep but narrow lot. Turning the house sideways gives it a front yard it would not otherwise have. Now it overlooks the neighbor's ample side yard.

Left: The den plays the old off of the new, both in furnishings and architectural details. The beaded-board paneling on the wall resembles porch ceilings in old houses, but it is new. The skylights leading to the kitchen enhance the contemporary atmosphere.

Above: Turning the house sideways on the small lot makes the site seem larger. What appears to be the front yard is really a neighbor's side yard. This orientation also places the greenhouse (at right) on the south side of the house where winter's heat gain is greatest.

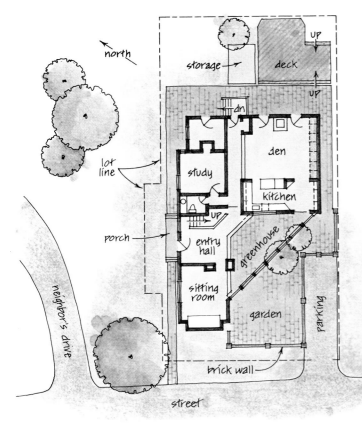

Above: Though new, the house (right) sits comfortably among its Victorian neighbors. Color, size, and materials help it blend into its surroundings, but details like skylights and metal chimneys and major design features like the solar greenhouse (at far right, not visible behind the brick wall) reveal it as truly contemporary.

A Louisiana Shotgun Lives for Today

A turn-of-the-century Louisiana shotgun benefits from the addition of a new rear wing, parking court, and pool area—all modern amenities but in keeping with the character of the original.

It began with a small frame cottage located in the town of Covington, Louisiana. The original house was fine as a cottage: compact, with well-proportioned rooms. But the owner needed a much larger living and dining area for entertaining. This prompted the addition of a large wing across the rear of the house, forming a T-shaped floor plan.

Above: The exterior color, a gray green hue from the Colonial Williamsburg reproduction paints, is contrasted with pure white trim. Lattice around the entire perimeter of the house softens the foundation.

Right: This frame house, a Louisiana shotgun built about 1900, comes alive with a new rear wing (left background) that adds a large living room and dining room on the first level and more bedroom space on the second. A raised deck and pool terrace fit within the L created by the new addition.

Above: The spacious living room opens up to the outside with tall French doors draped for shade when necessary. Raised cypress paneling was added to bring rich, architectural detail to a house that was originally void of any decoration.

On one side of the wing is a sumptuous living area. Many of the furnishings are from the fine reproduction collections of Williamsburg, Charleston, and Savannah, giving a feeling of formality. But that grand tradition is relaxed by the lavish use of color—the owner has used deep, rich colonial colors that are usually associated with the upper South rather than the

Bayou country. But their richness seems right at home in the more tropical area of south Louisiana.

To provide off-street parking, a motor court was located on one side of the new addition, easily accessible to the front door and to a side service entrance. On the side opposite the parking area is a landscaped pool with deck.

Above: At one end of the living area, a large paned window brings in an abundance of light. Luscious furnishings of velvet and leather make an inviting area in which to sit and relax.

Left: This sunny sitting area, adjacent to the kitchen, is part of the long side corridor that once connected the public spaces of the house with the more private rear areas. A large expanse of paned glass flanked by French doors gives a view of the pool and deck beyond.

11

Settling into Texas Traditions

The sheltering porches of a typical Texas farmhouse inspired this new home. True to its region in both style and materials, it seems to have grown steadily for years—like the live oaks around it.

On the edge of San Antonio, three limestone chimneys poke from a grove of live oaks. They stand as landmarks on a hilltop—and hint at the house that is nestled below the trees. The stone house is long and low, with porches tucked under its steep metal roof. It rambles like a Texas farmhouse that has been added to over the years.

The indigenous style which inspired this new construction consists of a central house completely ringed by porches. Parallel wings were added to either side, encompassing sections of the porch. Each of the three parallel sections is staggered to place the house carefully on its site. In the end, only a handful of trees was removed.

In addition to the regional architectural style, area materials such as limestone walls and tile flooring add to the feeling that the house is several generations old. But this is no mere copy of history. Porch columns, for example, are cast concrete. "You need some counterpoints to keep the native elements looking their best," says the architect.

Above, right: The path to the front door winds between trees and over an aqueduct that returns clean water to a swimming pool. Water bubbles from the fountain at right.

Right: The trees that hug the entrance to the house appear to have grown up around it. Along with the historic style of architecture, they give the house an appearance of having been here a long time.

Left: The living room ceiling rises to 18 feet with exposed trusses, and a skylight runs the length of the ridge. The expansive room opens off a short hall. The same resawn cedar used elsewhere is on the hallway walls; a reproduction Windsor bench stands against one wall.

Right: Walls are made of limestone. The ceiling and the end wall are resawn cedar lightly stained gray. D'hanis floor tiles are made south of San Antonio.

Below: With a large pane of fixed glass on one wall, the front entry feels as open as the adjoining porch.

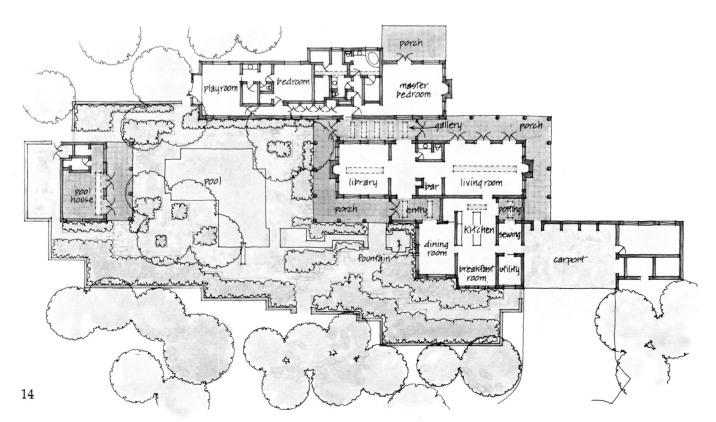

14

Above: A gallery leading to the bedroom wing is also designed to recall an enclosed porch, using the same tile, wood, and stone as the entry. Skylights bring extra light into its center.

Left: The library and the master bedroom have floor-to-ceiling "windows" that open onto the gallery. These interior windows provide the two rooms at the rear with a view through the house to the trees in front. The window style of one-over-one (fixed glass above and single sash below) is typical of a nineteenth century farmhouse. Bedroom windows have louvered shutters for privacy.

15

Family Life-Style Produces Tennessee Farmhouse

Southern values traditionally placed on family gatherings and relaxed living are inherent in this rambling country home on Signal Mountain, Tennessee.

Above: A large, open greatroom is the hub of activity. Aglow with the warmth of wood, the room resembles the inside of a log cabin with exposed beams and a hearth used for cooking.

Above, top: Suppers are served family style in the dining room at the Georgian pine lazy-Susan table. The huntboard against the back wall was originally used to serve food outdoors to mounted horsemen.

Warmth and personality—this new version of a traditional country farmhouse has both. "We wanted a place for our children and grandchildren to visit often. That called for plenty of space both inside and out," recall the owners. The heart of the house is a 24- x 28-foot greatroom complete with kitchen. Exposed fir and pine rafters in the greatroom converge with a larger middle support beam called a summer beam. This type of construction was particularly useful in building colonial farmhouses, since it is simple to erect but gives maximum strength.

A large open hearth, traditional symbol of pioneer family life, dominates the wall at one end of the greatroom. An antique trammel is fastened inside the fireplace opening with an antique crane across the back, and the family uses the hanging pots there to cook beans, stews, and cornbread.

Fir "gunstock" posts (simple boards that flare at the top) frame the hearth on both sides. The posts are copies of a colonial wall treatment used in the corners of a dwelling. The firewood holder is a hollowed-out poplar stump, once used to cure salt.

The owner did all the trim and millwork by hand. Having researched Early American patterns used in molding, he fashioned a dado to make the kind of cut he wanted. His handwork as well as the many antiques and recycled building materials make this a well-loved house full of family memories.

Right: The kitchen, at one end of the greatroom, utilizes rafters to display a collection of baskets. Across the back wall hang antique cast-iron pans still used for making cornbread.

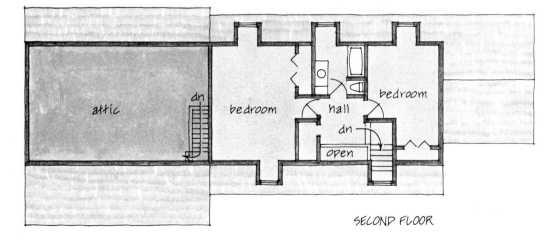

Far left and above: The exterior of the greatroom looks like an original structure to which a larger wing was added later. The photo on the right is of the larger portion of the house, taken after the siding has weathered for several seasons. A split-rail fence in front of the house emphasizes the contour of the land.

attic

dn

bedroom

hall

bedroom

dn

open

SECOND FLOOR

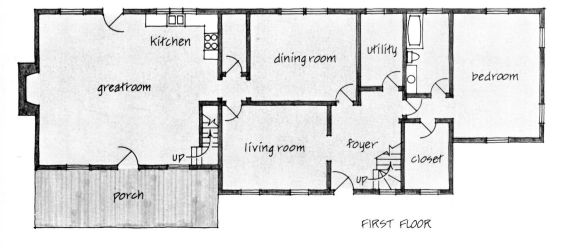

kitchen

dining room

utility

greatroom

bedroom

UP

living room

foyer

closet

UP

porch

FIRST FLOOR

A Warm Welcome from History

This new house in Charlotte, North Carolina, captures some of the exuberance and eccentricity of a Victorian country house. But for all its charm, it lives like today.

The owners of this comfortable, informal home re-created the spirit of a Victorian country house—but in a contemporary design. Now they have a home that has the feeling of lively Victorian architecture but is flexible enough to meet the family's constantly changing needs.

The house itself is an assemblage of parts, reminiscent of the circular towers and bays of the nineteenth century style. In the true Victorian spirit of excess, some of the round openings are not operable windows at all, but decorative circles cut into sections of wall with large, square expanses of fixed glass set several feet behind.

Even new features have details that recall the old. The deck on the rear of the house is certainly a contemporary feature—though its curving wall has a hint of Victorian pattern in its band of fish-scale shingles. Likewise, the kitchen is a long galley for efficiency's sake—but it ends in a bay window that echoes Victorian shapes.

In addition to capturing the essence of Victorian architecture, the house does contain pieces of genuinely old architecture. Nonstructural beams that crisscross the living room, den, and master bedroom were taken from the walls of a dilapidated 1840s log farmhouse. Unadorned doors to closets, pantries, bedrooms, and bathrooms came from old farmhouses; a finely detailed front door, pair of living-room doors, and back door came from stylish Victorian houses.

Left: This house is a bright spot in the woods at night. Its shingled form looks like a carriage house or a hunting lodge; its round chimneys bring to mind circular Victorian towers.

Above: A frame of log beams separates the dining room from the den. The pine floors here and in the living room were milled from the timbers of an old train trestle.

Right: In the master bedroom upstairs, antique beams frame the bed like a sleeping alcove. The simple doors on the closets came from old North Carolina farmhouses.

Far right: The kitchen is a narrow galley that ends in a Victorian-style bay window. Its counter tops look like conventional butcher block but instead are laminated oak strips intended for use on the floors of truck trailers.

Above: From the entry hall, the deck and woods are in full view through large panes of fixed glass and a circular cutout in the outside wall. The bands of rounded shingles, which ring the outer edge of the deck with a fish-scale pattern, continue on the round chimneys of the house.

Above, left: The living room is crisscrossed with beams that came from an 1840s log cabin. Furnishings are a mixture of antiques, including a collection of porcelain plates and a sofa (at right) that was purchased from a barbershop.

Far left: A generous deck is one expression of the contemporary life-style the house accommodates. The house design is an updated version of a particular Victorian mode, the late nineteenth-century shingle style.

25

A House and a Half

No other area of the country enjoys such easy access to recreational waterways, and homes on the water represent a distinctive part of contemporary Southern architecture. Here's just one innovative solution.

Much of the pleasure of a beach house is sharing it with friends and family, but too often, privacy is at a premium. This North Carolina coastal cottage is actually two tiny houses instead of one: one for the adults and a second smaller hideaway for rambunctious teenagers or visiting friends.

The larger cottage is a simple, 600-square-foot box topped by a hipped roof, with one of its gable ends facing the water. The smaller, 300-square-foot cottage has a simple shed roof that takes its angle from the roof of the larger cottage.

Above: A long boardwalk leads from the beach cottage to a small docking area in the shallow waters of the sound.

Right: This playful cottage on Bogue Sound is comprised of two separate little houses for a total of 900 square feet. Lots of glass facing the water brings views and abundant light to the interiors.

Above: For privacy, the cottage has no windows or openings on the street side. A walkway that goes under a partial arbor leads to the rear deck and to the entries of the two separate buildings.

Left: The angled deck that joins the two cottages is used as much as the interiors. With shady places all day long, it is great for anything from breakfast to entertaining in the evening.

The small deck that serves as a connector between the two structures juts out on an angle toward the water. The deck wraps around a multistemmed live oak, making an important union of house with landscape.

Building costs were kept to a minimum by use of standard building materials. Exterior siding stained a light gray is at home with the driftwood and oak trees that surround the cottage.

Left: Fixed windows were made from standard-sized sliding-glass door panels. Above the windows is a large half-circle of glass, an interesting architectural feature allowing views of the trees.

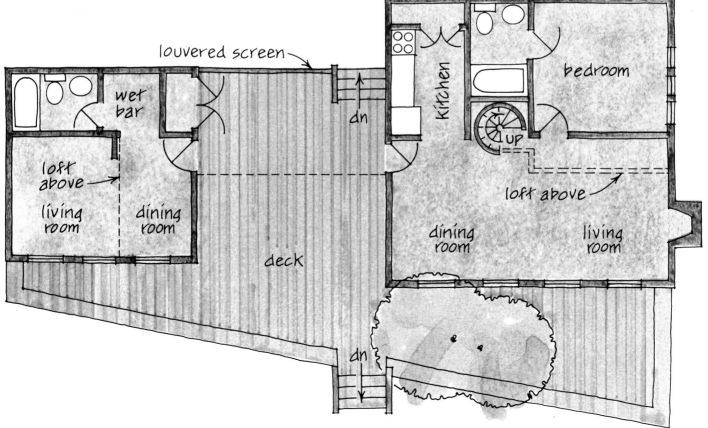

Turned to the Outside

This traditional house exemplifies a regional respect for the natural environment. It is a small, first home, but seems larger for its close relationship to the out-of-doors.

Over a creek and up a winding, dogwood-lined driveway, this house seems like a secluded retreat. But in fact, it is in an established Birmingham neighborhood, a few blocks from major shopping areas and thoroughfares.

A ravine, creek, and steep slopes were primary reasons why this lot remained undeveloped over the years, despite a prime location. But a young couple, both landscape architects, saw the potential and, with help from an architect, designed a house that makes the most of its natural environment.

Since the slopes are extreme, parking and turnaround space was the most limiting factor. The most level area was set aside for cars; the house was built on what remained. The parking area also determined the front door location—at the side of the house.

The owners wanted guests at the front entry to be able to see all the way through the house to

Right: Exterior and interior building materials were chosen to blend with the surrounding woods. The gray brick was salvaged from an old building downtown and used on the outside for its weathered appearance. Where shiplap siding is used, the wood is painted a soft gray.

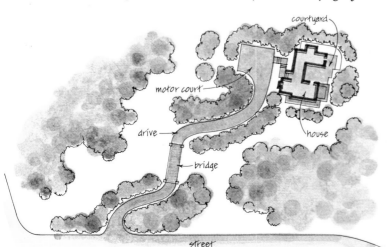

SITE PLAN

Above: The house forms a U around a central brick terrace, which is used for entertaining almost all year long. Spring, summer, and fall have proven great for large parties. "We leave the doors open when the weather is good and guests just wander in and out," say the owners.

Left: A gallery porch with ceiling fans stretches across the front of the house, overlooking a dogwood-studded slope and creek beyond.

an outside view beyond. To achieve this, French doors were placed opposite the entry. They open onto a brick terrace. The house forms a U around this important outdoor space, with public rooms on one side of the U and private quarters on the other.

All of the interiors are oriented to outside views. Each room has either long, oversized windows or 9-foot-tall French doors. A screened porch off the living room and a gallery across the front of the house extend the living space during warm weather, and year-round, these porches make an important connection with the surrounding woods.

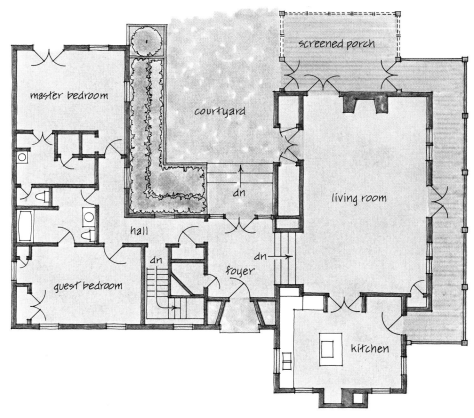

Above: The living room is light and open with a tray ceiling that rises to 13 feet. On the right of photo, doors lead to the gallery porch across the front of the house.

master bedroom

courtyard

screened porch

living room

hall

dn

guest bedroom

dn

foyer

dn

kitchen

Adding to Your Home

As the family grows, it may appear that an addition is the obvious solution. But the design of the addition can be an innovative solution to your family's special needs. This is how it can work.

Finesse in a Large Addition

When the addition is half-again as large as the original house, a smooth integration is critical. Similar materials and construction complement the existing house.

In cities across the South, growing young families enjoy living in picturesque older neighborhoods. They often find themselves faced, however, with houses that were built in an era of small bedrooms and tiny closets and in a day when family rooms were not in vogue. The only solution may be a major expansion. This Birmingham couple used a well-designed plan to add not only a great deal of space but also a new easy livability to their home.

A two-story addition on the rear made possible a spacious family room downstairs and an enviable master bedroom and bath upstairs. The genius of the new plan, however, according to the family, is a second, back stairway. "Before the back stairs were built, there always seemed to be a bottleneck at the single staircase in the house. Now it's much easier for our family to move through the house."

Above: Dentil molding under the eaves, painted brick, and roof slopes were repeated in the large rear addition to visually link it to the existing house. The result is an addition that looks like part of the house and not like new construction.

Left: The rear addition was held to one side of the deep lot so that a usable garden space was retained. The brick terrace is now as private as a courtyard. French doors open from the new family room onto the terrace.

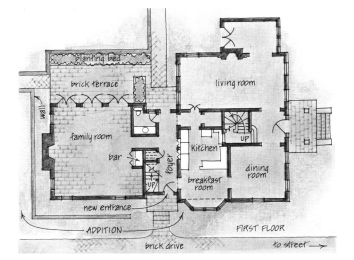

FIRST FLOOR

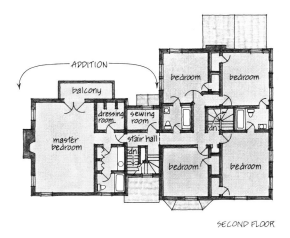

SECOND FLOOR

Right: The owners wanted the new family room to contain one antique architectural feature and found this weathered mantelpiece in South Alabama. The rough texture and bleached color of the mantel are repeated in baskets and other accessories.

Far right: Upstairs in the master bedroom, windows on three walls admit plenty of light. Paneled shutters can be closed in cold weather to help retain heat. French doors lead to a balcony overlooking the terrace. The room was painted bottle green to contrast with the natural color of the walls on the first floor.

Below: French doors, which open onto a sheltered terrace, give the family room a spacious, open feeling and allow views of trees and terrace inside.

38

Small Addition, Great Impact

A new 5-foot-wide gallery across the rear of a typical 1950s house in Houston seems to double the space. Now there is a view from almost every room.

Sometimes what is needed to make a floor plan livable is not an extra room or two but an unexpected space that opens up the house. This Houston home had a predictable four-bedroom, two-bath floor plan with small windows and unimportant door openings to the exteriors.

To improve traffic flow and bring in the light, the architect proposed a 5-foot-wide gallery across the rear of the house, with several sets of sliding-glass doors forming the exterior wall. Improved circulation, light, and views have replaced the once-dark, closed-up interior spaces.

Above: The gallery hallway improves traffic flow and opens both the family room and three bedrooms to views of the rear deck and pool area. The original exterior walls of the bedrooms (now interior wall of the gallery, seen in left background) were replaced with sliding-glass doors having small-slatted adjustable blinds. Open, the bedroom doors offer a direct view across the gallery to the rear garden. But the blinds covering them can be closed for privacy without affecting light and ventilation in other areas of the house.

Right: A whimsical circular opening at one end of the gallery provides a long view from the breakfast nook beyond. A settee with a Southwestern look provides a place for reading or relaxing.

Above: The family/living room now looks out onto the shady arbored deck, giving an open, airy feeling to the once closed-up room.

Above: The floor-to-ceiling glass of the gallery creates a visual link between the pool and house. The slatted arbor over the deck helps to shade the gallery during the day.

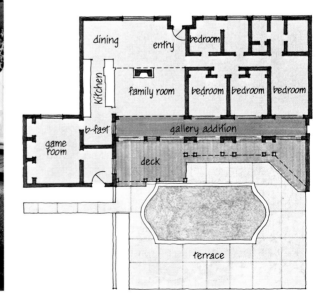

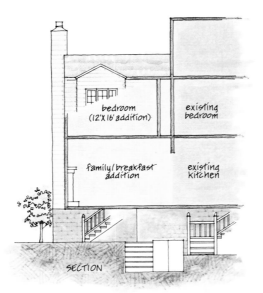

SECTION

Here's Where the Family Lives

This sunny two-story addition at the rear of a traditional house opens up the kitchen, offers views to the garden, and creates a country setting. It is the hub of family activity.

Much of the exterior appeal of this new construction comes from projecting elements which break up the two-story mass. For example, the chimney, which steps out, keeps the addition from appearing too narrow and adds architectural importance to the end wall. A boxed bay projects from the second level, framing the window beneath and adding substantial scale to the side of the addition. The small roof overhang above the entry reaches up toward the existing house to help bridge the gap between old and new. It also forms a small, cozy niche of an entry with some protection from the weather.

Inside, the existing kitchen seems larger now that it spills into the family room. A new cased opening was cut into the kitchen wall to open it to the new family room.

White walls in both spaces offer a neutral backdrop for the warm, primary colors of furnishings and artwork. Around the family-room walls, close to the ceiling, is a stenciled vine done with a brushed technique for a muted appearance. The colors in the pattern echo many of the colors used elsewhere.

Left: This two-story addition at the rear of a traditional Atlanta house has the charm of a small cottage. Since the site slopes toward the back, the addition is built on a high brick foundation to raise it to the level of the existing first floor. The door to the addition now offers a convenient entrance, close to rear parking.

Right: The existing kitchen is left much as it was, but cabinets were freshened with a rich blue-green paint and new hardware. An island, located between the kitchen and family room, serves as work space and a place to enjoy light meals. Just beyond the island, a large breakfast table can accommodate the entire family.

Above: A large cased opening was cut into the wall of the existing kitchen to connect it with the new family room.

FIRST LEVEL

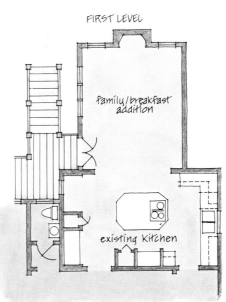

family/breakfast addition

existing kitchen

Right: A living room with master bedroom above was added to the rear of the house at right, and a single-story sunroom was added at left. The large living-room windows and French doors leading to a balcony off the bedroom give views of the bay. The bedroom is sheltered by a mansard roof, which minimizes the addition's size by blending with the shingled roof of the original house. The mansard design also allows the addition to have a nearly flat roof that does not project above the roofline of the main house, so the addition is not visible from the street.

A Cottage that Grew, but Stayed a Cottage

The new owners of this bayside home in Virginia Beach expanded it to hold a family of five—without giving up its cottagelike charm.

Even before they bought it, the owners of this house knew it was too small for their family of five. But they also knew houses were seldom available along this stretch of Virginia Beach's Linkhorn Bay.

"The lot was what sold us," they recall. "We just loved the view. The decision to buy was a matter of whether we could make the house large enough." They could, with the help of a Norfolk architect who doubled the space and improved the view, without sacrificing the original cottage style.

One key to the successful remodeling was the flexibility of the owners, for the architect's plan changed the use of nearly every room. The den became the kitchen; the old kitchen and dining room were combined into a larger dining room; the living room became the study; and a side porch became a guest room. A garage with bedroom above was added to the front. But the most important changes were on the back—facing the bay. Here, the architect added a sunroom that has two walls of glass. And a new living room with master bedroom above also faces the bay.

Above, top: A bright new sunroom with two glass walls is a casual family space. The adjoining kitchen was formerly the den.

Above, right: Interiors of the new living room are muted to make the view of the lawn and bay outside even more dominant.

Left, bottom: A garage was added on the street side at right, but the main house still keeps its cottage look. From the front, the second-story bayside additions cannot be seen.

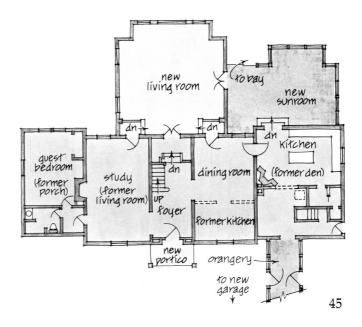

45

A Sensitive Addition to History

Years after its initial restoration, alterations are still being made to this old Savannah home. They suit the changing needs of new owners without disrupting the home's historic architecture.

Above: The family-room interior is traditional in its detailing but contemporary in its use. A television and stereo are kept in built-in bookcases that flank a fireplace, and the room's sofas open into beds for guests. Stairs at the far end lead to a playroom below. The ground floor of the addition incorporates the playroom and extra storage with the kitchen and family room on the second level.

Above, top: The new kitchen and family-room addition to this 1796 Savannah town house is at right, replacing an old garage. Its materials, design, and size blend well with the house.

This particular house is well known in Savannah. Guidebooks and tour buses regularly point it out as the city's haunted house. Like most other owners of old homes, the family must live with the various spirits of architectural history. While they enjoyed the character of the house, they were haunted by its functional shortcomings.

The first time the new homeowners had a dinner party in their historic Savannah home, they discovered the kitchen was so small they had to stack dishes on the back stoop after clearing the table. "All I needed to do to cause confusion in the kitchen was open the refrigerator door," recalls the hostess.

Today, the old kitchen (which was originally a butler's pantry) has become a wet bar, and a combination kitchen and family room has been added to the side and rear of the house. Seen from the street, the 34- x 14-foot addition is barely noticeable. The exterior is covered in lap siding that matches the siding on the original house. But it adds a family room and kitchen on the second story, and much-needed storage and a playroom on the ground level. Traditional but casual, the addition blends well with this eighteenth-century home.

Right: At 9 x 10 feet, the new kitchen is actually one foot shorter than the old one. But the storage, the counters, and the open plan make it radically different. Counters now ring three sides of the work area, and the 9-foot peninsula has cabinet doors on both sides. The kitchen is open both to the new family room and to a breakfast bay, built by a previous owner. The floor-to-ceiling bay and a wall of sliding-glass doors in the family room overlook the rear garden and provide the kitchen with a view to the outside.

Before You Build

Remodeling or adding onto a house is a popular and practical alternative to moving. But be sure to plan the job before beginning work. Here are some guidelines.

Improving an existing house is an increasingly popular alternative to moving. Regardless of the type of improvement, there are some important points to consider before beginning work: how the planned improvements will affect the value of your home; how much of the cost you will recover if you decide later to sell; what zoning restrictions must be observed; what permits are necessary before construction can begin.

HOME VALUES

Improvements to your home will usually, but not always, increase its value. This fact is of interest to you if you decide to sell the house, and of interest to the local tax assessor if you stay in the house. Not only will improvements usually increase the resale value of your home, they will usually increase its appraised value also. As a result, your property taxes will go up.

The first, and perhaps most important, question to face before improving an existing house is whether or not the planned improvements will mean a house overbuilt for its neighborhood. Real estate values for home resale are based to a great extent on the values of neighboring houses. If an addition or other substantial improvement is made to a house that is already the most expensive house in the area, the improvement will have little effect on the resale value. Conversely, if improvements are made on a house that is surrounded by more expensive homes, the value of the improved house will usually increase by an amount equal to the cost of the improvements.

If you do sell your house, the dollar return on money spent for improvements will depend on what specific improvements are made. Adding new living space, adding insulation, modernizing a kitchen, and adding a central air-conditioning system usually produce the greatest percentage increase in house value, ranging from 60 percent to 100 percent of the cost of the improvement.

Converting attic or basement space to family rooms or bedrooms usually produces much less of a return on the money spent for improvements (30 to 50 percent). Special-interest items such as greenhouses, decks, and patios often return at resale only about 25 cents for each dollar spent on improvement. It is important to consider these figures and weigh the cost of the proposed improvement, the possible future return of home-improvement dollars spent, and your family's immediate needs and desires. An architect or builder can give you an idea of what improvements will cost; a local realtor can give you an idea of house prices in your area.

ZONING

Zoning laws vary widely across the South, and what is permitted in one city may be against the law in another. Check with your local zoning board (listed in the telephone directory under the city government) before you begin any improvements that will affect the outward size or shape of the house.

Most communities have minimum setback ordinances that limit the area of the lot on which you can build. These setbacks are at the front of the house, both side yards, and at the rear of the lot. Generally, you can add on to your house or even build a new structure as long as the addition does not extend outside the setback lines.

If you do want to extend your house beyond the setback lines, chances are you'll need a variance from the local zoning board. Your local building inspector should be able to tell you for certain if you need a variance. The procedure for obtaining a variance varies from city to city, but generally it involves presenting a plan of the proposed addition to the zoning board or adjustment board. In most cases, neighbors will be notified and allowed to voice any objections to your proposal. The zoning board listens to both sides and studies the effect of the addition on the neighborhood, and then makes a ruling either to grant or refuse the variance.

Besides additions, other types of improvements may be regulated by local zoning ordinances. For instance, attic remodelings often incorporate low, sloping ceilings, and many cities have minimum ceiling height requirements. One typical ordinance requires that at least half of each habitable room have a ceiling height of 7 feet or more. In some cities, even enclosing a front porch or carport requires a hearing before the zoning board. Opening a business in the home or adding rental apartments are also covered by the local building codes, and will require a hearing before you are allowed to proceed.

If you do need to ask for a zoning variance, talk to your neighbors first. Having them on your side or at least aware of what you want to do will be most helpful when taking your case before the zoning board.

BUILDING PERMITS

A building permit is required by most cities for almost any type of remodeling or new construction. The cost of the permits, which are available through city or county building inspection services, is usually based on the planned cost of the improvement. Ten dollars is a typical price for a building permit for a simple remodeling job.

If you are using a contractor for the remodeling or addition, he will usually obtain the permit for you. Make sure the permit is obtained and posted before work begins.

After construction begins, a local building inspector will make at least one visit to the project to make sure the construction meets local building code standards.

SELECTING A CONTRACTOR

Hiring a contractor to do the improvements will naturally cost more than doing the work yourself. But the contractor can usually do the work quicker (important if the addition involves opening up the house to the weather). Using a contractor is a necessity if you lack the experience or tools to do the job.

Contractors who do home remodeling or additions can range from individual craftsmen who do most of the work themselves to large construction companies whose crews of workmen specialize in various building trades. A small one- or two-man operation might be less expensive due to its reduced overhead and give a more personal touch to the work, but they will probably need to call in subcontractors for plumbing, electrical, and heating work. Larger contracting firms, on the other hand, may be able to provide more comprehensive service, especially on a large or complex job.

Regardless of the size of the contracting company, the important thing is to find one that can do the work required at a price you can afford.

If you are working with an architect or interior designer, he can be of considerable help in recommending reliable contractors. You can also check with friends, neighbors, local lending institutions, or building materials dealers for possible names of contractors.

Check to be sure that each contractor is licensed to practice in your city. Also ask for, and check, the references from any builder you are considering using. See what other homeowners thought of their work. Did they complete the work on schedule? Was it satisfactory? Would they use them again?

You should request bids on the remodeling from at least three of the contractors that you have determined to be qualified. Basically, this should consist of each contractor visiting the site and reviewing the working drawings and specifications. Remember that each bid should be in writing and should spell out the exact scope of the work and the total cost of the improvements.

If you feel all of the contractors are equally qualified, you can simply choose the lowest bidder. However, be wary of a bid that is far lower than the others; this may mean that either he is planning to take some shortcuts or that he has left out some part of the project.

OBTAINING A CONTRACT

No work should begin on your house until you and the contractor have signed a contract. This should include the specific services to be performed as described in the working drawings and specifications, the precise amount to be paid for these services, as well as how the payments are to be made.

Terms of payment will vary, but usually the contractor will require a down payment, particularly if he needs to order large items, such as kitchen cabinets or storm windows. However, the homeowner should not pay more than 25 to 30 percent of the total amount of the contract at first.

Here is a realistic schedule of payments to the contractor: 10 percent when the contract is signed, 10 percent when work begins, 20 to 25 percent when the job is a third finished, 20 to 25 percent when the job is two-thirds complete, and 20 to 25 percent when work is completed. The final payment should be held for 30 days in case there are any problems. This schedule allows the contractor to purchase supplies as needed but keeps you from making full payment until the job is done.

The contract should also include both a starting and a completion date. You may wish to require a penalty payment of a set number of dollars per day if the contract goes past the date set for completion. However, many contractors will hedge their bids somewhat to protect themselves in such a case.

Also, it is a very good idea to require in the contract that the contractor carry liability insurance in case anyone is injured on the job, as well as insure the work under construction, but you should check to make sure a policy has been issued.

Bay Windows Add More than a Little Space

A bay window almost magically transforms an ordinary room into a bright sunshiny space—it may even add a small amount of floor space.

Sometimes, all that a room (or even a whole house) needs is a little more space added in just the right place and in just the right way. Bay windows, in all their various forms, can add a much-needed few square feet of floor space and, more importantly, bring in the light and open out to the view. By borrowing visual space from outside, even the smallest bay will help make the room seem larger. Likewise, the added natural light will make the entire room feel larger.

A bay that extends just 2 or 3 feet out into the garden gives a dramatic effect, because you see the garden all around you. It puts you outside without opening a door. In the winter, a bay located on the south side of the house becomes a cozy spot throughout the day as the projecting glass catches the sun early, during the midday, and in the late afternoon.

Outside, nothing has quite the impact on a plain house exterior as a bay window. It becomes a focal point where there was none; it gives dimensional relief to a flat wall.

But another virtue of a bay window addition is what it does not do to the room. Since it is frankly an addition, matching the bay to the rest of the house is much less of a problem than with the more usual types of additions.

While a bay window lets you extend a room out 2 more feet without destroying the room as a conventional addition would, it is about a third the cost of moving the whole wall out. The materials of the bay do not have to match those of the rest of the room, eliminating the problems of matching new materials with old. For example, the original wall line provides a logical place for a change in surfaces, perhaps from wood flooring to tile in the bay. On the exterior, a glass bay is compatible with most siding materials.

TYPES OF BAYS

Bay windows come in a variety of styles; the three main types are the angled bay, the box bay, and the bow window. The familiar bay window features angled side panels that give it a faceted look. The box bay's straight side panels provide the maximum amount of added floor space for a given-width window and the maximum width of glass across the center panel of the window. Since almost any size of side panel can be used, the box bay can be extended out from the house farther than the other window types. A variation of the box bay uses solid side panels to direct the view straight out to the garden. The gentle curve of the bow window makes it a good choice for wide feature windows where only a slight projection is desired.

Roofs for bays also can take several forms. Small, awninglike roofs of metal or shingle are most often used on angled bays. A simple shed roof is the usual choice for box bays; often it is glazed for a greenhouse effect. If the existing roof of the house overhangs the bay, it can serve as the roof for the bay, usually with considerable cost savings.

The smaller box or angled bays usually are simply cantilevered out from the side of the house; sometimes decorative brackets are used. Larger bays often are extended down to the ground with a conventional foundation. A bay window of any type located on an upper floor is called an oriel window.

Often, small bays are the height of standard double-hung windows, allowing space for a window seat or plant shelf inside. The larger bays usually extend to floor level, providing a walk-in bay with space for chairs and a table.

INSTALLATION AND ORIENTATION

Adding a bay window is one of the easiest of additions. Often, you can simply remove the existing windows and replace them with a bay of the same size. For a bay that extends to the floor, you can usually lengthen the opening without any structural problems.

However, widening an existing opening to accept a wider bay window will often require reinforcement of the header over the window opening and also cutting away the existing brick or wood at the sides. Usually, you will have little trouble finding a bay window to fit an existing opening (*see sketch*). For example, to fit a wide opening, two or more stock units can be joined side-by-side to form a wide center section. The side windows of the bay can angle more or less steeply to vary the fit. For angled bays, 30 degrees and 45 degrees are most common; some manufacturers also list 60-degree units.

Above: Adding another 5 feet to the length of the dining room, this bay addition now allows the dining table to be extended for large dinner parties. Day to day, a smaller circular table and a pair of chairs sit within the bay.

Left: the box bay cantilevers from the house to clear a utility easement running close to the foundation. Multi-paned windows match the traditional styling of the house.

51

With any type of bay, it is best to have the side window units operable for cross ventilation; this will also leave the center units free of screens for an uninterrupted view. Casement, awning, or double-hung windows can be used for the units that are operable.

As with any type of window, proper orientation will help prevent overheating in the summer and provide some passive solar heating in the winter. A location on the south side of the house will gather maximum heat from the low-angled winter sun. In the summer, the sun is more nearly overhead and will be blocked out by the roof.

A location on the north side of the house, however, will give a soft, diffused light since it will admit little direct sun. A location on the east will let in the morning light and is an excellent choice for a breakfast area.

Since a bay window on the west would let in a lot of hot sun on summer afternoons, it is the least desirable choice for a bay window location. If you must locate a bay window on the west side of your house, shade it with deciduous trees or an arbor to help reduce heat gain throughout the summer.

WINDOW TREATMENTS

Finding a suitable window treatment for a bay is often a problem. The simplest, and often best, solution is to use no window treatment at all, perhaps just hedges or walls outside for privacy. Where privacy or light control is needed, there are two basic approaches: treat the entire bay as one large window with draperies or curtains that can be closed to completely cover the entire opening; or treat each window unit of the bay as a separate unit.

Shutters, blinds, or shades can be fitted to each segment of the bay, allowing complete closure or shading of any part (for example, to block the afternoon sun coming in the side of a south-facing bay). Some window manufacturers even offer double-glazed windows with thin-slatted blinds set between the layers of glass. These blinds can be adjusted for the desired degree of light control or raised completely out of sight.

Left, above and below: The opening of this south-facing bay was once occupied by a flat aluminum-and-glass window. Not only does the bay expand the living area, but it also provides wraparound views to the secluded rear garden. Outside, insulated wooden windows and fir panels wrap the box bay, which is supported on posts like a deck. Three windows facing the garden are fixed in place; casements to each side open for ventilation.

Above, left and right: Projecting out only a foot, this three-window addition gives just enough extra space inside to make the area above the sink a special focus for the kitchen. Casement windows at each side swing open for ventilation.

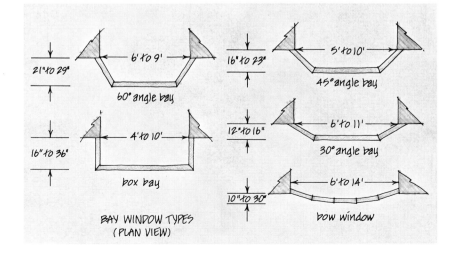

21" to 29" — 6' to 9' — 60° angle bay

16" to 23" — 5' to 10' — 45° angle bay

16" to 36" — 4' to 10' — box bay

12" to 16" — 6' to 11' — 30° angle bay

10" to 30" — 6' to 14' — bow window

BAY WINDOW TYPES
(PLAN VIEW)

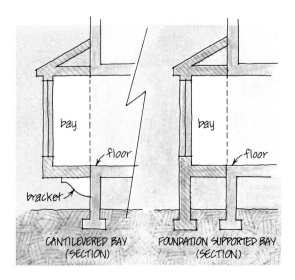

bay
floor
bracket

bay
floor

CANTILEVERED BAY
(SECTION)

FOUNDATION SUPPORTED BAY
(SECTION)

There Is More than One Way to Gain Space

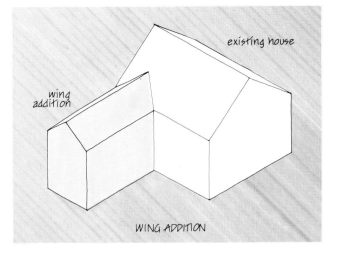

WING ADDITION

I f you are thinking of adding on, there are several ways to increase the living area in your house, and each has its advantages and drawbacks. Remember that not every type of addition works for every situation. For best results, use these comments only as guidelines when working with a design professional.

AN EXTENSION

Extending your house outward may seem to be the simplest form of addition, but it can be one of the most difficult. A good extension does not look like an addition at all. The problem is matching materials to avoid the added-on look.

Getting a good match often involves finding a siding material that is no longer made or trying to match new brick with old. Inside, structural requirements may call for a beam or header that could interrupt the visual flow from the existing house to the addition. The extension addition can also affect the proportions of your house—both inside and out—for better or for worse. Therefore, it is often best to make the addition a separate room or rooms, rather than an extension of an existing room.

An important consideration with an extension, as with several other types of additions, is how it affects circulation in the rest of the house. Often, the room next to the addition becomes little more than an oversized hall. Attention to traffic flow, door location, and furniture placement can prevent, or lessen, this problem.

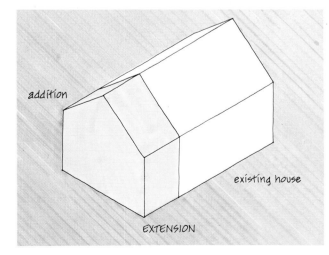

EXTENSION

A WING

Adding a wing at right angles to the main portion of your house can gain extra space inside and also define space outside for a terrace or deck. Because it joins only one section of the house, a wing does not usually block light and views the way an extension often does. Also, the size and proportions of the wing are not dictated by the size and shape of the house. For example, you could add a smaller, one-story wing to a two-story house. The exterior materials can change too if they are visually compatible with existing exteriors.

Another advantage of a wing is that it can be turned, for a different orientation from that of the rest of the house, to take advantage of a view or to face south for passive solar heat gain in the winter.

A SATELLITE

A satellite addition is a freestanding structure linked to the house by a narrow hall connector. Since only the narrow connector touches the house, the floor plan of the house is usually not drastically affected. Also, this type of addition does not block light from windows in the existing house. Because it is somewhat separated from the rest of the house, the satellite addition is a good choice for a noncompatible use such as a noisy place like a playroom, or a quiet retreat such as the master bedroom or a home office.

As with the wing addition, the satellite addition and its connector can also define or screen an outdoor deck or terrace. Matching the exterior materials of the addition with those of the existing house is less of a problem than with additions that attach directly to the house.

You may already have a satellite building, such as a garage, which can be converted into living space but would require a connector addition. The connector may be as narrow as 4 feet if used only as a passageway; it should be 8 feet or more to accommodate seating or dining.

A LEAN-TO

When a small addition is needed, the lean-to offers an easy and often economical choice. Since existing window or door openings often can be used to connect this addition to the rest of your house, the other rooms are usually not disturbed as much as by other additions.

Often a prefabricated greenhouse unit can become a surprisingly economical addition. And small lean-tos, such as bay-window units, can be cantilevered out from the house, eliminating the need for a foundation. (*See page 50 for "Bay Windows Add More than a Little Space."*)

With additions that are predominantly glass, be sure you pay particular attention to orientation to avoid excessive solar heat loads.

ATTIC EXPANSION

One of the most economical ways to add space is to more fully utilize existing space in your house, and the attic is a good place to start. Since the roof and floor are already there, an attic expansion usually involves just finishing the interior, adding or improving the stairway from the floor below, and adding or enlarging windows. Dormers, gable windows, or skylights can bring in light and views. Storage can fit into the low areas under the eaves.

However, not all attics have roofs pitched steeply enough for sufficient head clearance, and your ceiling structure may not be strong enough to serve as a floor for an attic room. For these reasons, it is a good idea to consult with an architect or engineer. Professional design help can also ensure that the dormers or other openings are compatible and properly located. If local zoning or setback regulations prevent a conventional addition, an attic expansion or a basement or garage conversion may be your only options.

A GALLERY

The typical gallery addition stretches the length of your house, yet is only a few feet wide. Since it serves primarily as a circulation space linking various parts of the house, a gallery can be as narrow as 3 or 4 feet. However, it should be wider if you want to use it for seating, dining, or other functions.

To keep the gallery from cutting off light to the rest of the house, many galleries are all or mostly glass. This also helps prevent the gallery taking on a tunnellike feeling. For privacy, a glassed gallery needs to be oriented away from the street or the more public parts of your site. Again, for passive solar heat gain, the gallery could be located along the south side of the house; a location on the west side will require screening to prevent overheating in summer.

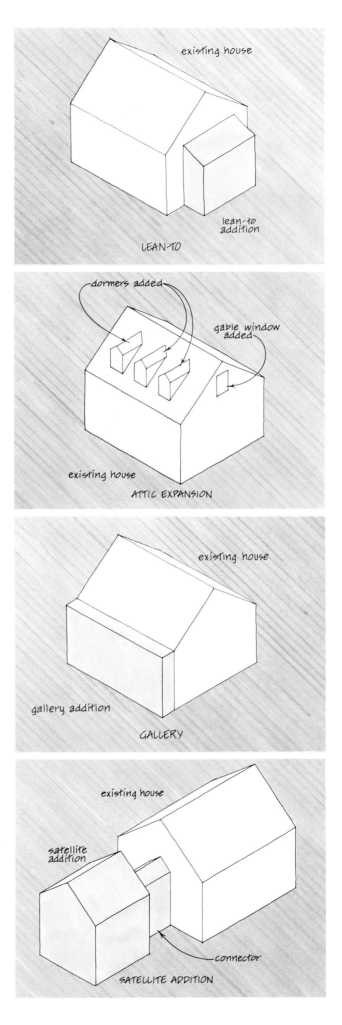

Remodeling

Homeowners once remodeled to "modernize." Now the goal is as likely to be to restore original character or to introduce charm where it is lacking. With the help of a professional, even an ordinary house can make a surprising transformation.

Remodeled?
No, Rebuilt

Taken down to its frame and put back together better than ever, this house comfortably blends traditional and contemporary elements.

The owners of this turn-of-the-century house in Charlotte's Fourth Ward spent most of their rebuilding efforts undoing the effects of time and previous owners. Their architect said at one point, "We stripped this house down to the 2 x 4s; you could stand in the front yard and see all the way through the house to Church Street."

Inside, the only things remaining original to the house are the heart-pine flooring and the stairs. This is not surprising since the house had at one time been carved up into ten apartments. Working every day for two years, the owners completed the remodeling themselves, producing a relaxed blend of contemporary cleanliness and Victorian ornamentation, with just enough of each for balance.

Right: The walls flanking the living-room fireplace stop two feet short of the ten-foot ceiling, creating a sound and light connection with the adjoining dining room. Ripping out old walls also took away the original trim and molding. Mantels and period window casings were recycled from other old houses.

Above: In the dining room, wallpaper, ornate chairs, and brass lamp evoke the feeling of an earlier era.

Left: Located above the living area, the master bedroom includes a study (through opening at right), and a new bath tucked behind the fireplace. As an example of the extent of the renovation, the existing brick chimney was pulled down to the ground and completely rebuilt to incorporate new, safer flues.

Far left: Although a new addition, the kitchen becomes very much a part of the house with the heart-pine flooring and salvaged oak beams. Oak cabinets wrap around the beams without touching for a light, floating effect. Red deck enamel on the base cabinets repeats the color of the stained-glass tulips above.

A Duplex Combined for Antiques

An older duplex, with undistinguished facade and interior spaces, had all the makings for an elegant single-family home. Now its contemporary, light-filled interiors are a beautiful complement to inherited antiques.

Above: The view from the dining room through the kitchen into the new family sunroom shows traditional pieces played against new materials and fresh colors. The door at right leads to the study.

Above, top: A porch on the front was enclosed to form part of the foyer; a new landing and brick steps lead to the front door. The dormers are softened with arched windows, matching those of the bay. The original asbestos-and-wood siding was replaced by stucco.

"When we first got married, we inherited a few fine antiques," explain the owners of this Montgomery, Alabama, home. This left the couple in a fairly typical situation: owners of some very traditional pieces but with a personal taste decidedly more contemporary. It was evident that combining the two units of a 1936 duplex was not only feasible but would create a place "to live in forever."

The original individual apartments were small (a little over 1,000 square feet each). The two kitchens were back to back. Now, one remains a kitchen, with improvements, and the other is divided into a downstairs bath and refreshment center. Second-floor changes were minimal. Two bedrooms were combined and one bath enlarged to form a master suite.

From the start, the owners knew they wanted the foyer to be special. The design team carved out a spacious entry that soars 22 feet to the roofline. It is here that the favorite heirloom—an imposing 9-foot-tall secretary made in 1830—commands immediate attention. "That's also the first thing you saw when you entered my grandmother's house," remembers the husband. Thus, the relationship between old and new greets you at the front door and follows you throughout the house.

Right: The foyer demonstrates the perfect blend of past and present design forms working together. The mahogany secretary anchors the space which soars to 22 feet.

Above: The rear deck fills the L formed by the new sunroom and the existing exterior wall.

Right, top: The living area, fresh with creamy walls and rust-colored accents, forms an updated backdrop for a large Victorian mirror above the fireplace. This entire wall, with built-in bookcases on each side, was designed around the mirror's proportions. Antiques are mixed with lighter pieces, such as the glass coffee table.

Left: The owners wanted one extra room at ground level—something more casual than the other living areas. So a sunroom was added to the back of the house, with access from the kitchen. One wall of the new room is glass all the way to the ceiling; floors are the same Mexican tile used in the kitchen.

new deck

new sunroom

refreshment center

kitchen

study

living room

dining room

kitchen

kitchen

dining room

porch

living room

living room

foyer

dining room

porch

BEFORE

AFTER

65

The Transformation Is Complete

Behind an ordinary facade, this solid, 60-year-old house hid an Italianate character. A complete remodeling brought it in line with the Mississippi tradition of romantic architecture.

This spacious, solidly built house had a lot going for it—large, open rooms, a deep shaded lot, and a desirable location in Jackson, Mississippi's, convenient Belhaven neighborhood. With extensive remodeling in mind, the owners consulted an architect. He was the first to recognize the basic character of the house as "vaguely Italianate" with the overhangs, proportion, and scale found in an Italianate structure dating to 1870 or 1880. His alterations—the tall first-floor windows, a wide porch, and decorative wooden moldings— highlight the Italianate lines, in keeping with many homes built in Mississippi at that time.

Left and above: During renovation, the original screened porch was replaced with a taller, open porch; slender wooden columns were used as more graceful supports. The modillions (supporting brackets) on the second floor were retained in the renovation; but the dormer was removed and second-floor windows were replaced with new ones evenly spaced to align with the new full-length windows on the first floor. Wooden-frame construction made it relatively easy to relocate window openings.

Above: Pilasters on interior doors were assembled from stock lumber and molding to create a visual link between the exterior trim of the house and the first-floor rooms.

Above: Weathered cypress paneling adds neutral color to the family room and kitchen, while Mexican tile provides subtle color underfoot.

Right: Soft gray on the walls and ceilings in the living room sets off the pilasters and deep crown molding, which were added to repeat some of the architectural details from the front porch. New floor-to-ceiling windows bring a sense of light and space to the room.

A Second Life for a '40s Duplex

Behind a new, refined exterior, the cramped rooms of this prewar duplex were reorganized into a more open, workable floor plan. It really is better the second time around.

A prime location, on a dead-end street in a better residential area of Greenville, South Carolina, made this property desirable, but the shingled duplex was generally considered a liability to be torn down. Or at least, that was the consensus until the new owners consulted a local interior designer. Now, the updated duplex has caused quite a stir locally—and quite a demand for older duplexes.

The first evidence of the skillful make-over is a new, refined facade. Neither existing entrance was convenient, so the owners opted for impressive double doors at the far left, nearer the driveway. Twin bays with full-length glass panels were added to relieve the unbroken straight line across the front of the house; they also bring more natural light into the living room and dining room.

Joining the two apartments with doors cut through the common wall was not enough to make a workable floor plan. Walls were eliminated and interior doors were enlarged to create a comfortable feeling of spaciousness.

There are still two baths, side by side. The owners joke, "We have the only house with one bedroom and three baths (counting the dressing-room sink)." But one great advantage is that it can grow with the family. The attic will be finished for children's rooms and the garage behind can serve as a guest cottage.

Above: Dark stain and copper-capped bay windows give charming formality to the new facade. False board-and-batten (4- x 8-foot rough-sawn plywood with battens applied) was added to the street side of the house. Original shingles left on the rest of the house were painted to match the smokey brown stain on the front.

Above, top: Special details make an impressive entrance: richly varnished doors, antique lanterns, and classical molding. The house number "11" is lettered in old-fashioned gold-leaf style. The feeling of elegance is continued in the foyer as well where black-and-white tiles suggest a formal marble entrance.

Right, above: Sunlight streams through the glass wall of the foyer, brightening both foyer and living room. Full-length panels of glass, used here and in the two bay windows, visually expand the formerly cramped interior spaces. For the same effect, interior doorways were heightened floor-to-ceiling.

70

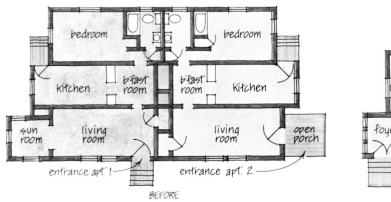

bedroom

kitchen | b'fast room

b'fast room | kitchen

bedroom

sun room | living room

living room | open porch

entrance apt. 1

entrance apt. 2

BEFORE

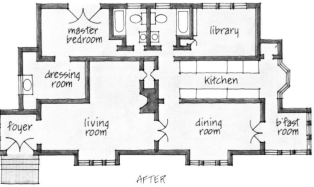

master bedroom | library

dressing room | kitchen

foyer | living room | dining room | b'fast room

AFTER

Putting the Best Face Forward

The front of the house can color your impression of the rest of it. Here are four examples to show what a difference exterior changes can make.

It makes good sense for a house to turn its best side to the street. Not only will the house look better, but it will be worth more, too. Each of the four older homes shown here were remodeled because their locations justified the expense. Sound structure and well-proportioned lines also helped make them good prospects. Taken together, a desirable location, solid construction, and sound proportions form the basis for successful exterior remodeling on any house.

In planning a face-lift, be sure not to underscale the architectural elements. There is a tendency when remodeling to make details—windows, doors, or whatever—too small. Remember the house usually will be seen at a distance of 50 to 70 feet.

FORMAL DETAILING

Architecturally, this house had good elements—for the most part, the remodeling mainly enhanced what was already there. The first-floor windows were extended to the floor, new shutters were added downstairs, and the paint colors were changed. Longer windows on the first floor make the lower section of the house heavier in appearance, which produces a nice solid-looking base. This also formalizes the house and gives it some character. A new front landing of coffee brown pavers gives importance to the impressive front door.

Originally, the house lacked convenient parking, and seemed, in addition, to be too close to the sidewalk. The new circular parking court in front provides a convenient entrance but also helps separate the house from the street. The court is basically square in shape with quarter-round corners and filled with river gravel. A long line of shrubbery planted at the sidewalk further separates the house and parking court from the street.

URBAN ELEGANCE

Originally this two-story house had a combination of shingles and siding for its exterior material. The frame house was completely stuccoed to give it a more elegant, urban appearance. The new house color, a soft mauve, was added into the stucco so the house would not need to be repainted in the future.

Quoins (masonry cornerstones) were added to define the edges of the new two-story entrance projection. They helped to accentuate the height, keeping the house from appearing too boxy. An existing entrance terrace was enhanced by changing the front windows to operable French doors.

Another important change was to combine three small windows above the door into one large arched window. The upper-story openings on either side of the central window are framed with small, usable iron-rail balconies. The balconies provide visual depth but also give protection to the French doors below. Recessed lights under the balconies illuminate the entry and terrace at night. A circular front drive was added to the existing side drive for guest parking. The circular drive also helps to formalize the entry.

UPDATE ON TRADITION

This was a typical 1½-story house. Though sound structurally, it had no distinctive looks to set it apart from others of its type. The three changes that made the big difference here were lowering the windows, sinking the drive, and providing a new color scheme. Each of these changes helped make a very traditional house more contemporary.

All the windows across the front were lowered to the floor for a more dramatic look and increased light and views to the interiors. Above the windows, for height and architectural detail, pediments or "eyebrows" were added. These are approximately 10 to 12 inches in height and built out of stock crown molding and lumber. The pediments are slightly wider than the window itself to keep from looking skimpy and to add balance for the new operable louvered shutters.

The new owners wanted a more formal approach to the house, so the side drive was moved to the center of the property and lowered about 2 feet. This gives a clear view of the house from the street and emphasizes the slight rise in ground elevation where the house is situated.

With the front entry given more importance, the door needed to be emphasized. This was done by making the door recess taller—it now goes all the way up to the roofline—and installing a pair of glass doors with a paned transom above. On either side of the door, heavier, wider pilasters replaced the original ones. An extra-wide brick front landing with low plantings on either side is in keeping with the new formality.

RETURN TO COTTAGE CHARM

Before remodeling, this house had false half-timbers and slight detail. Its paint colors contributed little toward defining the lines of the house, which had something of an English cottage look. Now a new face-lift makes the entry more important and introduces paint colors and new windows that are more appropriate to the lines and character of the house. New double doors with beveled glass for sparkle create a friendlier entrance with a slightly bowed stucco "eyelid" over the door to frame the entry and provide protection from rain.

Fake half-timbers were removed, and the body of the house was painted a soft, romantic melon. Creamy white trim helps to accentuate the shape of the house.

Altering all of the windows on the front of the house has made a big difference. Two square dormers were replaced by three smaller dormers that have arched windows and pitched roofs, more in keeping with the cottage style. Replacing a large central window with a projecting bay added dimension to the front of the house. Small, metal casement windows across the front were made longer by lowering the opening and adding fixed-glass transoms above them.

Landscaping the front and improving parking were also part of the remodeling. The drive, originally along the side of the house, was moved to the front with a pull-off for guest parking at one side. All foundation planting was removed and replaced with a solid mass of liriope, which forms a nice dark base for the house to rest on.

A House Raised to New Heights

This major remodeling effort to save a house built on a flood plain resulted in looks akin to a Creole cottage. It began by lifting up the house six feet.

It was incredible. I left for work one morning and when I returned, there it was, up in the air," the owner remembers. Thus begins the saga of what turned out to be a remodeling adventure.

They had lived in their house for about four years and loved the in-town neighborhood—just a few minutes from downtown Atlanta and close to major shopping centers. Like so many who decide to remodel rather than move, they

Above: This house was raised six feet off the ground to protect it from floods. In the process, it obtained a front porch, wooden siding, and architectural details—in short, personality.

Left: At the back, a new room was built on either side of the house. Between the two, a deck spans for outdoor entertaining space.

Above: A multipaned window replaces a large single-paned window behind the sofa in the living room.

preferred the stability offered by an older community: long-established friendships, large trees, and lush, mature landscaping.

The house itself was a well-built but basically plain three bedroom/two bath brick. But its lack of distinguishing features dimmed in comparison to its major drawback. It was built in one of the flood-plain areas common to the South; the owners knew it was only a matter of time before disaster would strike. Though the interior had never been underwater, flood waters had been too close for comfort many times.

It was during one of those close calls that they got the idea of raising the house several feet off the ground. After conferring with an architect to determine if the structure was suitable for raising, they hired a crew who specializes in house moving.

Preparation for lifting the house took about four days. Rails were extended beneath the floor joists (a house must have a crawl space in order to be lifted) and actually cranked up in about a day. New foundation piers were put in to support the house. Afterwards, lattice was added to fill in the space left between ground and house.

As long as the house was being raised, they decided to give it a face-lift also. The Creole-looking raised cottages around Mobile provided inspiration. Again with the guidance of the architect, the family opted to replace the exterior brick with wooden siding painted a soft gray. A new porch gives dimension across the front.

Since individual bedrooms were very small and there was no family room, the owners added a 15' x 25' room on each side of the house at the rear. One wing opens off the dining room and gives casual living space. The other wing forms a spacious master bedroom suite. Both new rooms open onto a deck that connects the new wings.

Above and bottom left: For this new family room, large windows were used to create a feeling of spaciousness. Tall French doors open onto a small deck that connects the new family room with the bedroom suite.

Left: By pushing out a slim box bay on one wall, these homeowners added a pleasing architectural element to the master bedroom. Adjustable shelves within the narrow side walls create a suitable niche for books.

A Guide to Remodeling

The successful case studies shown in this chapter prove that remodeling can accomplish a lot. But the process can be overwhelming. To make your own remodeling go more smoothly, here is some sage advice from those who have been through it before.

With unpredictable interest rates on new mortgages and the high cost of new construction, many people are choosing to stay where they are—and improve their present home. Established neighborhoods in good locations and the opportunity to customize a house to meet family needs are additional reasons to keep your existing house. But like everything else about home-ownership, any type of major remodeling should be carefully considered and planned.

It is important to decide whether or not you want to stay in your present neighborhood, and to assess how much your remodeling will add to the market value of your home. Checking building codes and zoning laws, selecting a reliable contractor, and drawing up a contract are all critical stages of the planning process. *(See "Before You Build" on page 48.)*

IF YOU PLAN TO SELL LATER

Here are some other remodeling considerations if you plan to sell your house in the future.

—Realtors, builders, and contractors agree that the kitchen and bath areas will sell a house. Although the kitchen need not have expanded floor space, it should offer efficiency. A dishwasher is the most sought-after appliance, while increased cabinet space and a continuous counter-top work area are also high on the list of priorities.

—While efficiency is more important than size in the kitchen, the same is not true of bathrooms. The current trend is toward larger and more luxurious baths, particularly those with dressing areas, twin lavatories, and adjoining walk-in closets. In most houses today, two full baths are preferable, particularly if three or more people live in the house.

—Adding a new room, such as a bedroom or family room, should be carefully considered since new construction costs more per square foot than remodeling existing space.

—In most cases, a swimming pool is not considered a positive selling item except in Florida and coastal areas.

—If your family needs a specialized area, such as an art studio, consider how this room will be viewed by future owners. Give the room features that will make it multifunctional and thereby adaptable to another family's needs.

MAKING THE MOST OF PROFESSIONAL DESIGN HELP

Getting professional advice on remodeling will probably save you mistakes and money in the long run. Interior designers and architects have the ability to visualize the overall effects of both architectural and decorating changes and can provide you with sketches so you will know what the completed remodeling will look like. In most cases, the result is a remodeling that is more functional and aesthetically pleasing than one that just happens.

Before talking to a designer or architect, decide how much money you can spend and what needs you want the remodeling to satisfy. The more guidelines you can give the designer, the more suitable the design will be.

PERSONAL VIEWPOINTS

It is important to consult with the experts. Talking it over with a designer and an architect made the difference. Owners, Greenville, South Carolina.

"Had we done the remodeling the way we wanted," says the owner, "the end results would not have been as pleasing." The family had a little-used screened porch (above, right) off their kitchen. Glassing it in and adding a small side deck to tie it to the rest of the house created a year-round living area. Its small proportions—the room is about 10' x 14' and the deck about the same—is a good example of how a well-planned small space can still be effective.

The expertise of the architect and interior designer added valuable insight to the remodeling. "We might have wanted to square off the deck with the house," explain the owners. "Instead, the architect suggested an angle with a peak—this draws you out visually into the woods beyond. Similarly, the interior designer used a large sectional sofa in the sunroom—probably larger than we would have used, but now there is seating for several people."

The interior designer sums up the project: "The main thing is complete understanding between the client and the designer. The owners and I would talk back and forth until we got down to what we actually did. That way, the design has lasting appeal, not just something that's faddish."

Get a designer involved early on. He (or she) can help with the small details that a builder might overlook. Interior Designer, Atlanta, Georgia.

"If a designer can review the plans before the builder's contract is signed—before things are finalized—some mistakes can be averted," says the Atlanta-based interior designer who worked on the attic renovation of this home. "Selection of light fixtures, location of outlets, choice of colors and other accessories—all these details will add up at the end."

The attic bath (right) was expanded to accommodate more traffic, while new double lavatories and mirrors make the most of space as well as light. At the same time, the ceiling was lifted to the roofline, and windows that follow the shape of the eave were added to bring in the natural light.

A primary goal for the designer or architect is to understand the client's life-style. Interior Designer, Birmingham, Alabama.

"Without knowledge of the unique personality of each client, you are not able to project any design image. The lady of the house weaves— that was important—and both she and her husband like 'old' things. Even so, they did not want an old look," comments the interior designer who worked on the remodeling of this 1950s ranch-style house (above).

The house needed a fresh, youthful look and room for some specialized interests. A large cased opening was formed on either side of the fireplace, giving a contemporary feeling to the combination living/dining room and the adjoining sunroom. Removing moss rock around the

fireplace left a sleek, small opening, which adds to the updated appearance of the room. New sliding-glass doors and new sidelights in the sunroom bring in abundant natural light.

"So many people have a hobby and try to hide it," comments the designer. "I didn't want to hide the loom—it's a handsome piece." With good light, the sunroom was a perfect place for weaving. "The couple also had a piece of an old quilt, a 200-year-old family heirloom. We enclosed it in glass and pulled color for the room from it," adds the designer.

The owners summarize their feelings about the remodeling: "We knew the direction we wanted to go—but not the specifics. Because our interior designer was careful to find out about our particular interests, we feel that the remodeling belongs to us."

Be realistic about the actual demands made on you during remodeling. Owners, Austin, Texas.

The bungalow still looks the same from the front; but the plan the architect designed for the back of the house provides an impressive amount of added living space (above).

It is important to work with an architect and a builder with whom you feel comfortable and trust—it is almost like finding a good doctor. Another suggestion is that one designated member of the family be available at all times to make unforeseen decisions that require an immediate answer. There will, of course, be times when mutual agreement is called for, but if only one partner deals with the contractor, there will be far less chance of a mix-up occurring.

"If we could do it again," these owners say, "we would go with a fixed price, even if it seemed a little too high." A builder known to be competent will give you a fair price but naturally will allow some extra margin to cover unexpected expenses or time spent on the job.

According to these owners, "We'd also put in some sort of daily penalty clause for not finishing the work on time. Allow extra time, allow extra money, but then be willing to follow through with penalties if it's necessary." Any remodeling seems to take longer than planned, but the projected date of completion should be put in writing.

"Do not make changes in the original plan once construction is underway, because a couple of hundred dollars here and there add up fast. Consider that labor is really about half the cost of remodeling," the owners caution.

And for those who do major remodeling, this final bit of advice: Move out, if at all possible, even if only for a few days. The clutter and confusion is so disruptive that sometimes it is best to escape.

Working with an Architect

Architects are trained to take a comprehensive look at buildings. How well do they fit into their neighborhoods? How do the elements—space, light, color, structure, and mechanical systems—combine to make the whole?

But that does not mean that they undertake only large-scale projects. You can take advantage of an architect's broad view of building for a small project—a house, a renovation, or an addition. Working with an architect can be especially helpful if you want a design that is uniquely your own or if your project involves difficult arrangements of spaces or uses, unusual structure, or difficult siting. By taking a comprehensive view, an architect can come up with solutions that might not occur to you.

SELECTING AN ARCHITECT

Certain concerns commonly arise, however, when homeowners consider hiring an architect. How do you find the right one? Will the architect be worth the additional expense? Will the architect try to talk you into a style you do not want?

Because architectural firms usually concentrate their practices on commercial and institutional buildings, you often will deal with one member of a firm or with an architect practicing by himself if you want residential design.

Only in the past few years have professional codes of ethics allowed architects to advertise, and the practice still is not very widespread. But you may find ads in the *Yellow Pages* or elsewhere, in which architects list their specialties— homes, renovations, or energy-conscious design, for example.

Another source is the local chapter of the American Institute of Architects (AIA), the professional association for architects. State capitals generally have an office, as do some larger cities. And while a professional organization may not recommend one architect over another, it will have rosters available of member architects. It may also have a file of architects' brochures, illustrating their previous work and providing information about firms. The AIA may even have lists of architects who have experience or interest in different types of buildings.

Membership in the Institute allows an architect to use the letters AIA after his name. It means that the architect subscribes to certain codes of ethics and professional standards.

Many competent architects—including young members of large firms, university professors, and government employees who do not depend on an active practice of architecture for their livelihood—are not members. However, these architects also take occasional commissions.

Other organizations also may be of help in finding an architect, especially if you have a specialized project. If you are restoring an old home, for example, you may find recommendations through a local preservation or historical society.

Contractors, builders, and other homeowners may recommend architects they have worked with in the past. Homeowners, in fact, may be your most valuable source, for they can tell you how an architect was to work with and what the completed building is like.

When selecting an architect, the single most important consideration should be the quality of his past work. Most architects have photos and drawings of their work available for you to study. If possible, visit some of the architect's buildings.

And if you are dealing with an architectural firm, be sure to meet the individual who will be designing your home. Architects usually describe designing a house as the most challenging and difficult of their tasks because so many details are personalized. So for architect and client alike, personal chemistry and effective communication are crucial.

WORKING TOGETHER

Making preliminary inquiries in no way obligates you to hire an architect. But once you make the decision, there are certain steps that must be taken immediately. The first is to determine the scope of the work. For while an architect's principal role is that of a designer, the profession in recent years has encompassed many specialties, such as energy efficiency. You may even want to hire an architect to help you select your lot.

Once you begin design, you will need to determine how detailed the drawings will be—will the architect provide just a rough plan or will he provide detailed construction drawings? Will the architect be involved in managing construction? It is important for the architect and owner alike to understand each other's expectations if the project is to run smoothly. AIA contracts are standard for spelling out the scope of the work and for determining pay, which is based on the work. These things need to be decided at the beginning.

Once you begin, there are other aspects on which you should be flexible. Though it can be helpful to have clippings from magazines or other specific ideas that you want included in your home, remember that the architect does not just draw plans for buildings. He will analyze your needs and come up with his own recommended solutions. He can include your ideas, but preconceived notions can prevent you from benefitting fully from the architect's expertise. Remember that effective communication, in fact, is essential to a good building from both architect's and client's standpoint.

THE FINANCIAL INVESTMENT

How much work the architect does determines how much he is paid. If you are uncertain over what the work is to be—especially in the early stages—you may pay an hourly consultation rate for a brainstorming session. Later, you pay per diem, a lump sum, his office cost plus a lump sum, or a percentage of the construction cost. Payment usually is made in several predetermined stages during the process. But remember, if you decide not to build, you must still pay for the preliminary work.

The architect's fees can vary widely, depending on your city and on whether you hire a firm or an individual. But you can typically expect to pay anywhere between 8 percent and 15 percent of the construction costs.

Will the total cost be more if you hire an architect? Sometimes it is, but not always. By analyzing your needs, an architect may be able to suggest alternatives you had not considered—perhaps an addition instead of a new house or a renovation instead of an addition. There may be solutions that mean not building at all. The architect may be able to suggest materials that are less expensive but still good-looking.

The way the building is put together will affect the cost, however. An architect-designed building may cost more because it is custom work. Even if you save money by doing a smaller job or by using simpler materials, you may spend the money later on labor. An odd-shaped deck, for example, may be more aesthetically pleasing than a square one, but the extra materials caused by angles and the extra labor involved may result in a final cost that is the same as or more than a larger, simpler design. Questions of expense and style and whether custom design is your goal will vary with each building and are best considered on an individual basis.

Further information about architectural services and fees is available from The American Institute of Architects, 1735 New York Avenue NW, Washington, D.C., 20006. Also, some of the state chapters of the Institute will provide information.

Working with an Interior Designer

Interior designers are a growing body of professionals trained in a variety of home-building and remodeling areas. An interior designer can help you save money and avoid costly mistakes by careful planning.

Designers can help you choose colors and fabrics; they can design kitchens and baths; they can help with interior door sizes and placement, and positioning light fixtures and outlets. In other words, they can help put it all together.

To begin with, trained designers are able to work directly with a builder or architect to make spot changes that add to the beauty of your home. Sometimes these changes do not cost a great deal more if they are done before construction begins.

The time to consult a trained designer is at the beginning—during the initial planning stages, whether you are building new or remodeling. At this point, changes and rearranging can be done easily.

Professional designers also have a number of resources at their fingertips. A designer has access to showrooms that are open only to those in the design field and often unique designs cannot be found anywhere else.

CHOOSING AN INTERIOR DESIGNER

Finding the right designer is simply a matter of choosing a designer whose work appeals to you. Reputable designers usually have color photographs of their work; sometimes you can see their work at actual sites by appointment.

If a friend cannot recommend a designer, check the *Yellow Pages* under the heading "Interior Designers." Several working in your area should be listed.

Designers who have had at least six years of experience in the field, including schooling, and have proven their skills in both written and practical tests are allowed to use the initials ASID after their name. Membership in The American Society of Interior Designers does not guarantee quality and competence, but it is another checkpoint in obtaining professional guidance. By writing to The American Society of Interior Designers, 730 Fifth Avenue, New York, New York, 10019, you can find an ASID member near you.

Remember, many excellent designers are not members of ASID, either by choice or because they have had too little experience to qualify.

WHEN YOU CONSULT AN INTERIOR DESIGNER

One of the most important things to consider will be the amount of money you wish to spend. Give the designer realistic budget guidelines.

After deciding how much you wish to spend, make an inventory of all your furniture and accessories. Sometimes a piece that you think the designer will throw out may be salvaged by refinishing, painting, lacquering, or re-covering.

Working with a designer can be a rewarding partnership. The designer often insists that the client get involved, contributing actively not only with selections but in a tangible way, providing material for special accessories. He will incorporate hobbies, needlepoint, artwork, and collections.

COST OF AN INTERIOR DESIGNER

Cost will vary from place to place and from designer to designer. Also, there are several different ways a designer can charge for services, including a flat rate, an hourly rate, a percentage of the merchandise, or the merchandise at cost plus 25 percent. The job itself, depending on its size and difficulty, may indicate the way fees are decided.

The hourly rate varies, but is usually anywhere from $25 to $50. An initial consultation in your home can sometimes last two or three hours. Most designers charge a flat fee of about $50 for this kind of consultation. Even if you do not use the services of the designer further, this kind of preplanning meeting can get you pointed in the right direction. After the consultation, should you want to continue working with the designer, the hourly rate will probably switch to some variation of the above-mentioned fee charges.

Some designers have their own specialty shop, but you are under no obligation to buy any of their merchandise. Some large department stores have designers who are available for consultation. They can answer a few questions for you; but if you want their help extensively, their fees will be similiar to those of an independent designer.

Drawing up a contract during the initial stages of design is usually a good idea. Then there are no misunderstandings about what the designer is expected to handle. Remember, however, that there are some aspects of interior designing that go beyond the control of your designer. Deliveries can be late or factories can be out of certain fabrics and furniture. But you can expect the designer to keep you informed on the status of all orders and to respond to requests as soon as possible.

Kitchens

The kitchen can be many things—a highly organized room planned for efficient cooking, or a relaxed and cozy space filled with antiques and warmed by earthy materials. Whether you are designing a new kitchen, remodeling an old one, or simply enjoying the one you have, it is likely that you will be able to adapt an idea from one of these kitchens.

Colorful Country

This kitchen proves that traditional need not be dull. Colorful tiles, deep red walls, and wooden cabinets create a lively warmth. It is country with color.

The cook in this Tulsa kitchen wanted a country look in her kitchen but one which also had a freshness and zip to it. What she had was a dark, narrow, uninteresting space. With an abundance of hand-painted Portugese tiles setting a lively remodeling pace, her traditional kitchen is now bright and inviting.

A few structural changes were necessary to open up the kitchen. The long narrow space was a problem, as there would be no way to widen the kitchen without going into great structural changes. They made a virtue out of the length and the narrowness when they removed the end wall and installed a long island. The 2-foot-wide island is, at 10 feet, considerably longer than the usual, but the counter-top space is convenient to both sides of the kitchen. Since the original kitchen lacked a dining space for the family, a small area with fireplace was added at one end of the kitchen.

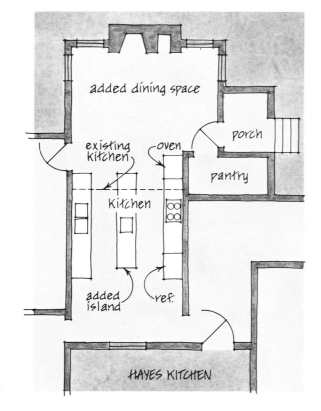

Above, left: Comfortable chairs at one end of the kitchen provide a place to relax. The cornice above the window consists of 1" x 10" board with small band molding at the bottom and 2-inch crown molding at the top.

Right, above: Splashes of color from hand-painted Portugese tile counter tops make an immediate impact in this remodeled kitchen, formerly a dark, narrow space. Capitalizing on the long, narrow space, the 2' x 10' central island provides work space and a small sink handy to both sides of the kitchen. Counter tops are covered with the same tiles used on the island. The dark-stained walnut cabinets are factory built and have a plate rail around the top.

Right: Russet wallpaper, brick, and dark-stained woods contribute to the traditional look of this kitchen. The end wall of the old kitchen was removed to open it into the new dining area.

Above: A generous, half-circle base cabinet, nicknamed the "grand piano," provides a buffet service somewhat removed from the working area of the kitchen.

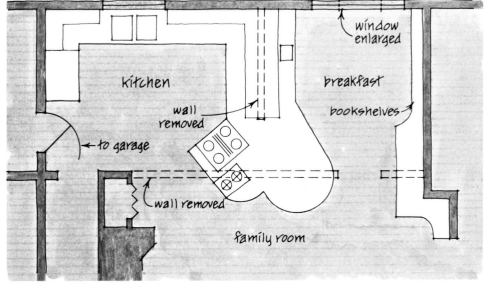

window enlarged

kitchen

breakfast

bookshelves

wall removed

← to garage

wall removed

family room

Bright, White, and Livable

White laminate brightens this contemporary cooking space—a spit-and-polish look for a kitchen open to guests.

I n a house on a shaded lot in Birmingham, Alabama, dark paneling and cabinetry created a dimly lit kitchen. So when the owners decided to remodel, white won out over color. By knocking out a wall and removing some overhead cabinets, they also opened the kitchen to the family room, which lightened the whole area.

The tour de force is a large, half-circle cabinet which reaches out toward the seating area. This one unusual shape makes a simple kitchen plan distinctive and helps to unite the two areas.

In a kitchen that is open to guests, easy-to-clean counters and cabinets are especially important. Durable plastic laminate was applied to all cabinets, both for its easy maintenance and its contemporary look.

Above: A wall was removed between the family room and the kitchen, opening the kitchen to the seating area and view of the patio beyond.

Left: A standard double-hung window was replaced by a larger fixed window to lighten the breakfast area. Floor-to-ceiling shelves were added to house the cook's collection of recipe books.

A Kitchen with Nothing to Hide

A potpourri of pots, pans, and other cooking utensils is displayed against natural wood beams. This is open shelving at its best.

I n a two-story Victorian town house in Richmond's Fan District, the kitchen was a dark, dingy room with little to offer. Since the young mother is an avid cook, she wanted everything easily accessible. The result is an unassuming informality that draws family and visitors to the kitchen.

The basic scheme for the remodeling was laid out by an architect friend, who admits, "Much of what was built was designed as it went up." The effect of this build-as-you-go resembles a child's construction-toy project on a grand scale: a network of natural fir and oak beams suspended from the ceiling and fastened together with carriage bolts.

To leave as much exposed as possible, the heating and air-conditioning ducts were not cased. In fact, the treatment was taken a step further, and the exposed ductwork was painted in bright greens, reds, and blues.

The refrigerator is encased in a natural wooden box, allowing the sides to be used for hanging aprons, towels, and pot holders. A double pantry with revolving shelves also helps utilize every available space.

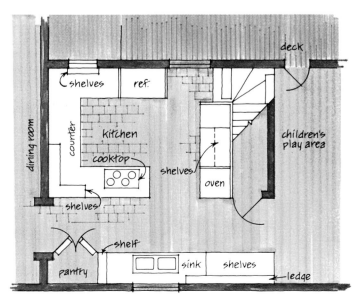

Above, left: Varying heights of shelves allow a place for everything. Breakables are stacked on higher shelves; pots and pans are grouped on lower shelves. For hanging utensils and small kitchen gadgets, cup hooks were used where practical. Strips of magnets are also used for scissors, knives, and other small metal objects.

Right: Open shelves—some suspended from the ceiling—give a friendly look of organized clutter to this remodeled kitchen. Exposed heating and air-conditioning ducts are painted bright colors in contrast to the natural wood tones of the shelving.

A Country Kitchen without Cabinets

Rustic tables and cupboards replace conventional storage units in this kitchen, giving it a friendly warmth and charm.

Not every kitchen needs built-in cabinets and counters to be well organized, functional, and attractive. This Cullman, Alabama, family removed all the pine cabinets from their kitchen, then enlarged the room and furnished it with antique tables, old cupboards, and new pieces of country-style furniture. They say now, "We really find it more convenient to have everything right at hand, and we've avoided all the wasted corners usually found in built-in cabinets."

"Furnishing a kitchen this way is really much less expensive than having cabinets constructed," the owners point out. "We already owned several of the primitive pieces we used here, and we bought the long counter table for very little. Our carpenter made the sink table for less than $75. So for just a few hundred dollars, we were able to get exactly the look we wanted." They did construct a large pantry across from the sink for extra storage space for groceries and cooking utensils and to conceal a dishwasher.

Left, top: This baker's cabinet once belonged to the owner's grandmother; now it holds a collection of pewter tankards and plates. The right accessories and small pieces of furniture work together to make this kitchen special.

Left: The owners used a quantity of old lumber to achieve the look and feel of old construction. The floor is surfaced in reclaimed heart pine, and the room is paneled up to the chair rail with recycled lumber.

Right: A carpenter built this pine sink table. The simplicity of the design makes it compatible with the primitive antiques in the room. Tins and wooden boxes provide decorative storage.

Above: Cabinets in this butler's pantry were the inspiration for new cabinets in the kitchen, a detail that helps restore the charm of this older house.

Kitchen Regains Its Older Charm

The butler's pantry inspired the cabinetry design for this remodeled kitchen, bringing about an authentic older look.

Although the butler's pantry had not been altered when an Atlanta family bought this 1920s house, the kitchen had been inexpensively modernized. As a result, much of its character was lost. To restore the feeling of an older kitchen, distinctive features of the cabinets in the butler's pantry were reproduced in the kitchen cabinets. The tall upper cabinets with pane-glass doors and the simple, heavy base cabinets in the kitchen closely imitate both the style and scale of the older cabinets.

Although the butler's pantry is now used as a breakfast room, the cabinets still retain their serving function between kitchen and dining room; the addition of a small sink in the base cabinets has updated the pantry as a wet bar. Again, for an authentic traditional look, a reproduction of an eighteenth-century fabric is used as wall covering and a table skirt.

The owner wanted a few authentic details that she would not advise for everyone. For example, the latches of the upper cabinets are installed above her reach for both authenticity and the most pleasing proportions. For someone who is less of a purist, she suggests a concealed magnetic catch at the lower part of the cabinet with the brass latches modified to a strictly decorative function. She also values the original hardwood floor enough to wax it regularly.

Above, right: Pane-glass cabinet doors duplicate both the style and scale of the cabinetry in the butler's pantry. A long search uncovered enough antique brass hardware for the new cabinets.

Right: Once used only for serving, the butler's pantry is now a breakfast room. The wall covering and a table skirt are a reproduction of an eighteenth-century fabric.

Let's All Move into the Kitchen

Comfortable furnishings make these three examples more than just kitchen/breakfast-room combinations. These special rooms invite people in.

"It's a pleasant place to be."

"I never knew a kitchen could be so much fun," says the owner of this plant-filled kitchen *(left)*. The room forms the core of the new house and functions as a hallway between the public spaces and the private quarters.

"We entertain a great deal, and a lot of times people just stay in the kitchen. I put food and drinks on the glass dining table, and there's enough room to mill around. It's a pleasant place to be."

The architect comments, "Our whole intention was to make it look like it's not a kitchen—perhaps as if the room were already there and someone just put up cabinets. That's why certain things in it look unexpected like the massive hemlock ceiling beams."

Left and far left: Mahogany cabinets and hand-painted tile counter tops give this Birmingham, Alabama, kitchen/dining area a special richness. The 12-foot ceiling gives the room a distinctive height.

99

Right: The gently angled island separates the kitchen work space from the family seating area but still allows an open view between the spaces.

Below: Though small, this family seating area off a Charleston kitchen has comfortable furnishings that give it the versatility of a larger room. Lunette transoms and center-hinged pane-glass doors bring light into the room.

100

"I'm proud of the kitchen area."

Before remodeling, this kitchen *(opposite page)* was not a favorite room. "In fact," one of the owners says, "we heartily disliked it. Nevertheless, at parties, that's where people would stay; I had to entice them into the living room. Now, I'm proud of the kitchen area."

The owners wanted to include an island in the remodeling. It aids in traffic flow and also allows a wall of cabinets down one side of the kitchen. Though the total area is only 400 square feet, there is space for a small table at one side for dining, plus a settee and chairs for lounging. The television and books are concealed behind louvered doors along one wall, and the washer and dryer are behind matching doors on the opposite wall.

"Now I can keep on cooking."

Surprise elements can help personalize a kitchen and add details not usually associated with this area. The architect of this kitchen *(right)* explains, "My clients wanted to enlarge their kitchen and convert a rear porch into a family area. I decided to incorporate a porch railing between the two spaces—keeping them slightly separate but allowing communication."

In addition to using unexpected details, knowing in advance how the area will be used helps determine many of the requirements. "I love to cook," says the owner, "and we wanted a place where family and friends could gather while I finished preparing the food—that's the kind of entertaining we do."

The architect used a rather large island (4 x 9 feet) to divide the work area from the rest of the room. The island has a sink and enough space for the cook to work while not being cut off from family and friends. The island does not have a hood or anything hanging above, which would have hampered the open feeling. The kitchen has two chairs with a small table in the immediate work space, in addition to comfortable family-room furnishings in the converted porch beyond. "My husband calls the kitchen area my command control center. I can run the whole house from here," says the cook.

Above: A large cased opening frames the connection between the remodeled kitchen and the new sitting room (foreground) of this Tulsa house. Beside the kitchen work area on an upper level, an 1820 fiddle-front Irish dresser and high-back chairs furnish a cozy spot for snacking or just visiting the cook.

Add an Island

Whether you are remodeling the kitchen or just giving it a face-lift, an island can make it more functional and attractive.

Too much floor space and not enough work space. You could walk yourself to death fixing a meal." That is the way one Southern homeowner described her old-fashioned kitchen, a big, square room with counters and equipment on the walls.

Building an island in the center of the room was the solution. It made the work area smaller and the kitchen more functional. At the same time, it provided extra counter space and gave the room an attractive focus.

A kitchen island can be as simple as a 2- x 3-foot butcher-block table or as elaborate as a 10-foot-long unit with built-in sink, cooktop, dishwasher, trash compactor, and ice maker. An island can serve merely as work space, or it can provide a place for casual dining as well. Our examples illustrate a few of the many possibilities that islands offer.

BRING THE FAMILY TOGETHER

This island in a Shreveport, Louisiana, home (left) is not just for the grown-ups. The whole family uses it.

Besides being the food preparation center for a remodeled kitchen, this 42- x 74-inch island also provides a place for the family's three children to snack and study.

The island is built of oak to match the existing cabinets. Its butcher-block top has an overhang on one side, making knee space for the three Windsor-back swivel stools. Brackets at each end support the overhanging section of counter top. On the working side of the island, three doors conceal storage areas. Included are a pull-out for canned goods, a bin in the center, and a pop-up shelf for a large mixer.

Left: This generous oak island matches existing cabinets. In addition to deep storage behind doors on one side, the other side features a bracket-supported overhang to allow seating on high stools.

Above: Bright, white tile shines on the surface of this 4- x 10-foot island. Even though the island is unusually long, a sink in the center keeps the work area compact. During parties, the island doubles as a large buffet.

ADD SERVING SPACE

The owners of this Houston home (above) stretched an existing island to twice its original length (now 4' x 10'). To do this, they moved an end wall out 4 feet.

One side of the island runs parallel to a blank wall in the kitchen. The space between the two serves as a circulation route through the house. During parties, this side of the island is used for serving, leaving free the other 2- x 10-foot half for food preparation. Although the island is unusually long, the location of the sink in the center of one side keeps the work area compact.

Storage drawers and cabinets along the serving side of the island hold silver, china, and linens; this is convenient to the dining and breakfast rooms. Beneath the working side are bins for vegetables, storage space for staples and mixing bowls, and a dishwasher.

103

MAKE ROOM FOR TWO COOKS

Because the couple that lives in this Birmingham home (left) loves to cook, it is not surprising that they added an island to the kitchen of their 10-year-old home. The cooks built the island themselves. It consists of a 24- x 36-inch butcher-block top supported by 1- x 2-inch slats. Shelves below provide storage for staples and pans.

Adding the island also made room for more storage overhead. Copper pots and pans hang from a simple acrylic rack. They are close to almost any part of the kitchen; and since the island blocks the floor below the rack, there is no danger of bumping into them.

SUPPLEMENT STORAGE

Originally this kitchen (above, right) was a tiny, dark room measuring only 8 x 10 feet. The adjoining dining room and breakfast room were also small. But when the owners ripped out the walls separating the three rooms in the 1920s Houston house, they gained a light, open area for cooking and dining. Without adding onto the house, they solved the problems.

Now the combined dining/kitchen area stretches 22 feet across the rear of the house. A round oak table is used for both family meals and for entertaining. The 82- x 64-inch island nearby contains sink and cooktop with dishwasher and ice maker located below.

In addition to the island storage, one end wall has been converted to storage. Three-foot-deep, floor-to-ceiling cabinets contain refrigerator, double ovens, and pantry. A buffet built in along one wall of the dining room also provides storage as well as display space for art.

The cabinets are surfaced in white plastic laminate to match the white-painted walls. Italian marble tops the island and buffet. For an interesting contrast, the hardwood floors are stained a rich brown. A geometric-pattern area rug defines the dining space.

CONSOLIDATE A LARGE SPACE

After a complete renovation, this kitchen (below, right) in Nashville is in about the same place as the original, but everything except the brick wall and window casings is new. A 42- x 150-inch island now fills the center of the room. Floor-to-ceiling cabinets, located at one end of the kitchen, provide plenty of storage.

The long island includes a double sink and a combination chopping board and warmer set flush with the plastic laminate top. A dishwasher is just to the left of the sink. Drawers and doors, finished to match the room's other cabinets, provide convenient storage. Along the other side of the island, there is plenty of room for casual dining.

Above: This small island, made by the owners, provides the additional work surface needed when both husband and wife want to cook at the same time. Adding the island made room for more storage overhead. Copper pots and pans hang from a simple acrylic rack, where they are accessible to both cooks.

Above: Italian marble tops this 82- x 64-inch island, which contains sink, cooktop, dishwasher, and ice maker in addition to ample storage behind laminated doors.

Above: A small kitchen, dining room, and breakfast room were combined to create a light, open area for cooking and dining. The round oak table is used for both family meals and for entertaining.

Above: The traditional style of this island matches the wall of storage beyond it and is appropriate to the original brick wall of a renovated turn-of-the-century house.

FIT AN ISLAND INTO THE
WORK TRIANGLE

Consulting an expert—an architect, interior designer, or kitchen designer—is a good idea if you want to add an island to your kitchen. But whether you work with a professional or do it yourself, you will still need to know some of the basics.

To be efficient, an island must be part of the kitchen work area. Most kitchen plans are based on three work centers: cooking, cleanup, and refrigeration. Appliances and storage and work areas related to each task are located close by.

An imaginary triangle connects the three work centers and defines the main traffic flow during food preparation. For maximum efficiency, the kitchen should be designed so that the triangle formed by the cooktop, sink, and refrigerator has a perimeter of not more than 22 feet. Too large a triangle will mean too many extra steps during meal preparation. If the triangle is too small, the result may be a tight and crowded kitchen.

If you want a large island that includes a sink or cooktop, it should be located at one corner of the work triangle. A smaller island that is only used as a work surface should fit along one side of the triangle. If it intrudes too much into the triangle, you will find yourself having to walk around it to get from one area of the kitchen to another. If the island includes a snack or eating area, be sure to locate that part of the island outside the work area.

If you are putting the cooktop or range in the island, try to provide counter space on both sides of the cooking surface. For ventilation, you can use either a ventilating hood or surface ventilation. Surface-venting cooktops usually carry cooking heat and odors away through an underfloor duct to the outside. Some manufacturers offer ventless models that filter and recirculate the air. Any separate ovens should be located in a wall outside the work triangle.

The sink is another work center that is often incorporated into an island. Such islands usually include a double sink with garbage disposer and counter space on either side of the sink. Located underneath are the dishwasher and trash compactor. Since the sink is used for washing and peeling fruit and vegetables as well as washing dishes, you may want to include a chopping block to one side. If you do not have room for a full-sized sink in a work island, consider installing a small bar sink to use for washing vegetables and as a water source for cooking. Put the big sink in a cabinet along a wall.

An island needs plenty of space all around for circulation; 3 feet on each side is a minimum. If more than one person in the family cooks at a time, you should allow extra space. You will also need to allow extra space for stools if you use your island for eating.

A good way to see what size island you can use is to make a scale drawing of your kitchen floor plan. Mark off the clearances needed around existing counters, cabinets, and circulation areas; then see what is left over for the island. For a more practical indication of the size island you need, make one out of large cardboard boxes. Walking around the dummy island for a few days will tell you if it is the right size for your kitchen.

If the space available is small, say 2 x 3 feet, consider adding a butcher-block worktable. It is relatively inexpensive and can be moved (some come on casters). If you have a little more space available, you might like to build an island that incorporates an eating counter as well as work space. For that type of island, you will need a minimum depth of 42 inches (48 inches is better) and 2 feet of width for each person that will be using the counter.

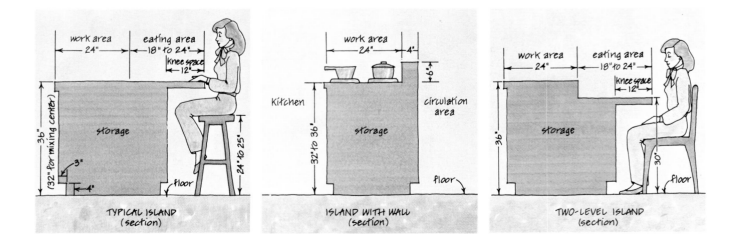

TYPICAL ISLAND (section)

ISLAND WITH WALL (section)

TWO-LEVEL ISLAND (section)

Islands, like other base cabinets, are typically 36 inches high. However, since this height is designed for people of average height (5'4" for women) you might like to make your counters slightly higher or lower if you are above or below average height. If the island will be used as a mixing center, a height of 32 inches is suggested. Many cooks have discovered that this height is considerably more comfortable for a cooktop.

If the island will be used for eating, you can make the surface the same level (around 36 inches) and use stools for dining. Or you can drop the eating side to a standard 30-inch table height and use chairs. Changing levels helps to define the two different use areas, but it also limits the work space, since it is rather inconvenient to use both of the levels during preparation of the meal.

If an island adjoins a main circulation path, you may want to consider raising the side next to the circulation area. A 6-inch or so raised wall will screen off any kitchen clutter. If the island is used for cooking, raising the side will also add a measure of safety—it will keep passersby from bumping into hot pots and pans.

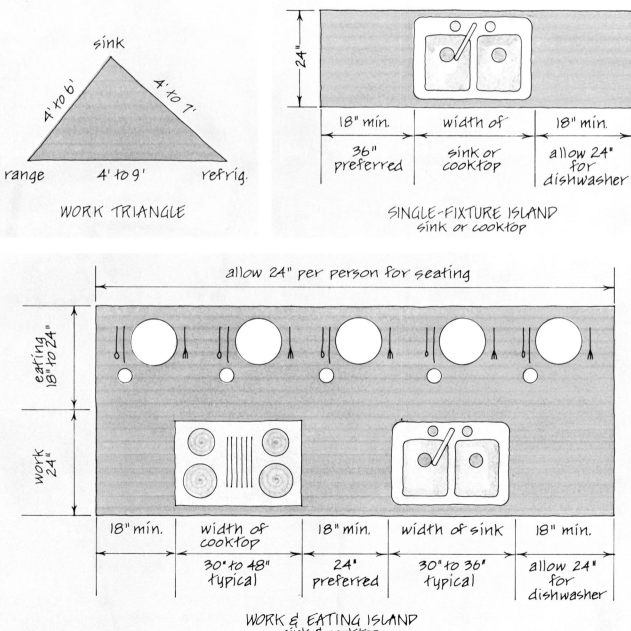

WORK TRIANGLE

SINGLE-FIXTURE ISLAND
sink or cooktop

WORK & EATING ISLAND
sink & cooktop

Planning Your Kitchen

The kitchen is the most complex room in the house. Not only is it a cooking center, it is the central storage area for food and cooking equipment and often a center of family activity. Two generations ago, before the advent of today's sophisticated appliances, cooking was hard, hot work and the kitchen was not a pleasant place to be. As a result, kitchen design was not very important to most people. But with today's interest in health and cooking—particularly gourmet cooking—many people spend considerable time in the kitchen simply because they enjoy being there.

Whatever your life-style and cooking needs, outfitting your kitchen properly is important. A kitchen must have the organization of a factory assembly line, the ambience of an artist's studio, and the warmth of, well, a country kitchen. Your kitchen should be designed for maximum efficiency but it should also reflect your family's attitude toward food and cooking.

Here is a quick checklist of the many decisions you must make when you build or remodel a kitchen.

PREPARING TO COOK/CABINETS

The largest item in the kitchen is the cabinets. And while cooking is the main function of a kitchen, you need ample space to store food and

Left: Natural-finish birch cabinets and butcher-block counter tops give this compact kitchen a light, airy feel. Base cabinets are white laminate trimmed with birch. Glass doors on the upper cabinets help make the kitchen appear larger. The shallow glass-fronted cabinet on the right is installed over a series of windows above the kitchen sink. Used for storage of glassware, these unusual cabinets provide privacy without cutting out light.

Right: A brass pot rack made from a curtain rod hangs over the work island in this remodeled and enlarged kitchen. The end wall was removed and a small porch enclosed using recycled French doors and leaded glass panels. The enclosed porch is now a breakfast area as well as a casual place for reading or television viewing. A butcher-block top is inset within the white laminate counter surface. Above the enclosed base cabinets, all storage is open, providing colorful accents against a clean white background.

Above and right: It is possible to paint varnished wood cabinetry and paneling without tedious stripping. Done by a professional here, the new white paint brightens a small kitchen, updating it without major remodeling. The end wall of the kitchen was removed and a small porch enclosed with white paneling to further open up the space.

110

cooking equipment. Storage is always working, even when you are not cooking.

As a general rule, there should be a minimum of 10 linear feet of base-cabinet storage and 10 linear feet of wall-cabinet storage. Allow more room for storage if you have a large family, prefer to shop less often, or do specialized cooking requiring extra equipment or ingredients.

Custom-made
Designed and made locally to fit your individual specifications

Specialized storage available

Higher cost than factory-made

Factory-made
Wide variety of styles and materials and specialized storage available (though not custom-made) at lower cost

Can have flexible components individually designed to fit your kitchen configuration

Wood
May be natural, stained, or painted

Usually traditional styling with moldings or other decorative panels

Contemporary styling with use of light natural wood or anodized stains in wood with no surface decoration

Laminates
Easy cleaning

More durable than wood

Can combine laminate-covered base cabinets with laminate-covered doors, with glass doors or open shelving above

Cost about one-third more than the same cabinetry in wood

Neutral colors safer than stronger colors if planning to resell house

Above, right: Deep cabinets run the full height of the ceiling to pack maximum storage into this compact kitchen. A shallow pantry on the end wall (not shown) provides space for canned goods and bottles. Cabinets and ceiling were painted a high-gloss, soft gray white to give the effect of a larger space. Cabinet doors extend below the bottom edge of the cabinets, making knobs or pulls unnecessary and thus preserving the clean look.

Right: Open shelving first became popular in contemporary kitchens, but now has found a place in traditional kitchens as well. Here a crisp, checked wallpaper sets off the rich pine cabinetry and simple pottery dinnerware on display.

Above: One special feature can have a big impact on the kitchen. A simple, brick fireplace adds rustic character to a kitchen with white walls and brown vinyl tile on the floor. A sloped ceiling and large skylights along one wall give the room a bright, open feeling and help to dramatize the soaring brick chimney. Incorporated in new construction, the fireplace opens to both kitchen and dining room.

PREPARING TO COOK/WORK AREAS

Ease of maintenance is the single most important consideration when selecting the materials and finishes for counter tops, floors, and walls. Constant use and constant cleaning require that kitchen surfaces be both durable and easy to clean. Smooth, continuous surfaces with a minimum of corners, cracks, and crevices will make the job of cleaning easier.

Counter tops
Plastic laminate
  Most popular surface available
  In wide range of colors at moderate price
  Can be wiped clean
  Damaged by scratching and scorching by
    hot pans
Stainless steel
  Durable, easy care
  Expensive
Butcher block
  Expensive
  Should not be used for chopping

Methacrylite
  Synthetic sheet material that resembles
    marble (Corian® one of the larger brand
    names)
  Available in white and limited other
    colors
  Integral sink of methacrylite is available
    and avoids installation joints
  Scratches can be sanded out
  Cost about two and a half times the cost
    of plastic laminate
Ceramic tile
  Durable, tiles easily wiped clean but
    grout joints between the tiles hold dirt
    and stains; expensive
  Items dropped on hard surface can break;
    tiles also can break
Marble
  Desirable surface for pastry cooks
  Sometimes inset within another material

Floors
Resilient flooring
  Usually vinyl, the most popular choice for
    kitchens
  Wide selection of color and patterns at a
    moderate cost
  Sheet materials have the advantage of no
    dust-collecting joints
  Tiles easier for do-it-yourselfer to lay
  Easy care
Hardwood floors
  Should be sealed with polyurethane var-
    nish (either mat or gloss)
  Probably will need refinishing every three
    or four years
  May wear quickly in the heavy traffic
    areas in front of the sink and range
Carpet
  Must be designed for kitchen use; ordi-
    nary indoor-outdoor carpet has porous
    backing that will let kitchen spills soak
    through
Brick, ceramic tile, and quarry tile
  Durable, but expensive
  Dishes dropped on them break easily
  Tiring surface to stand on for long periods
    of time
  Surfaces should be sealed to prevent
    spills from soaking in and staining
    the tiles
Cork and rubber
  Softer, easier on your feet than brick or
    ceramic tiles
  Comes in squares
  Cork presealed with a vinyl finish
  Rubber has raised dots; the lower the dots
    the easier to clean

Above: A peninsular work counter, containing a drop-in range, divides the work area from the dining area which is decorated in a relaxed country style. The suspended pot rack is constructed of dowels within a 1 x 4 frame.

Left: With the kitchen work area located on the front corner of the house, sloping skylights were a better solution than conventional windows. The skylights open the room to light and out-side views while still providing street-side privacy. Open shelving above the butcher-block counter top is con-structed of painted lumber, held together with plastic corner chips.

Walls
> Paint—gloss or semigloss enamel, easier to clean
> Wallpaper—specify washable

Lighting
General illumination most often from ceiling-mounted fixtures
> Incandescent
>> Lower initial cost
>> Warmer, more flattering color
>> Smaller fixtures, easier to install
>> Best choice for white kitchen
> Fluorescent
>> Greater operating efficiency
>> Less heat build-up
>> Avoid with white cabinets, unpleasantly cool and blue

Task lighting for counter-top work surface
> Incandescent downlights can be used over sinks or islands with no wall cabinets above
>> Recessed into ceiling
>> Flush mounted (track lights)
> Fluorescent mounted under wall cabinet

Plumbing Fixtures
Sinks
> Size
>> Double sinks—cooking and cleaning can be carried out simultaneously
>> One and a half bowls—in addition to the large bowls, a small one holds the disposer; frees main bowls from food scraps so they can be used for other tasks
>> One bowl—some sinks only have one bowl, which is larger than half a double sink; this allows you to clean larger pots, and the overall dimension is smaller so the kitchen has more available counter space

Left, above: This 3-foot-square opening is not a pass-through in the traditional sense but an interior window that opens the breakfast area to a view through the foyer to the outside. In a compact kitchen, a built-in banquette was tucked under the stairs to provide a place for casual dining.

Far left and left: A punch of red brightens this gallery kitchen in a converted condominium. The red tube is not merely decorative but houses a fluorescent light strip. Black laminate cabinets and butcher-block counter tops are set against a white tile wall.

Materials
> Stainless steel
>> Will spot if not wiped dry
> Enamel on cast iron
>> Comes in colors that may be matched to other appliances (Colors may go out of style, however, or new owner may object to color that does not match his appliances)
>> Can be chipped
>> Less expensive than stainless

Faucets
> Controls
>> Separate for hot and cold water
>> A single lever
>>> Single lever controls temperature and turns water on
>>> May be operated with your wrist when your hands are full
>>> Temperature may be preset

COST

Because of the equipment and plumbing, remodeling, adding to, or designing a new kitchen invariably creates the most expensive room in the house. An extensive kitchen renovation involving new cabinetry and equipment can easily cost over $15,000.

This brings up perhaps the most important question to ask yourself: Will this substantial investment produce a house that is overbuilt for its neighborhood? Adding an expensive kitchen to a house that is already the most expensive house in the neighborhood will increase the resale value only slightly. Adding or remodeling the kitchen of a modestly priced house that is surrounded by more expensive houses will usually provide a return of most of the money invested in the kitchen if the house is later sold.

If you are redoing a kitchen on a budget, here are some ways to keep the cost down.

—Keep the sink and other plumbing in their original locations; relocating plumbing lines is expensive.

—Utilize existing cabinets, if possible. Refinish or repaint wooden cabinets as necessary; plastic laminate cabinets sometimes can be recovered with a new color or pattern of laminate; metal cabinets can be taken to an automotive body shop and spray painted.

—Use open shelves wherever possible, thereby saving on the cost of cabinet doors.

—Store pots and pans on an overhead rack or wall-mounted pegboard. This will almost always cost less than enclosed cabinetry.

—Use standard cabinetry rather than the more expensive custom-built units.

Family Rooms

Whether a cozy, intimate space or a light-filled room, this is a place to show off family hobbies and interests, collectibles, and inherited family pieces. Known as the place for relaxation and sharing, these comfortable rooms sacrifice nothing in style.

It's Just One Wonderful Room

An unused carport provided the space, but a dramatic addition and country furnishings turn the room into a fun place for the whole family.

It was just wasted space." That is how the owners used to describe the carport at their Baton Rouge home. But the carport is no longer wasted. Remodeling, which included a shallow addition, has turned it into a special place for the entire family.

A 12-foot-deep addition, complete with fireplace, runs along one side of the remodeled carport. The ceiling of the addition soars to follow the roofline of the house, rather than matching the low ceiling of the original carport. During the remodeling, a study was converted from attic space over the carport. The high ceiling allows light into the study and gives the family room a bright, open look.

An old family home in Jackson, Louisiana, provided the rough-sawn beams and the beaded ceiling. Country antiques from the South and from Europe help create an informal feeling.

Floor-to-ceiling bookshelves and a box bay window now fill the original carport opening. The family dining table is centered in front of the bay to take advantage of the view.

Left: The dramatic fireplace was patterned after one in a Louisiana plantation kitchen. A multipanel wall of glass wraps around the fireplace. Since the window wall faces east and overlooks a heavily wooded swamp, window coverings are not needed.

Above, right: Country pieces give the room a relaxed, welcoming touch. For example, the cocktail table is an English pine table with the legs cut down. The table's rounded corners and distressed surface make it both safe and practical for a room used by small children. "The kids can't do anything to it that hasn't already been done," the mother points out. An old bar from a St. Louis hotel fills one corner of the converted carport.

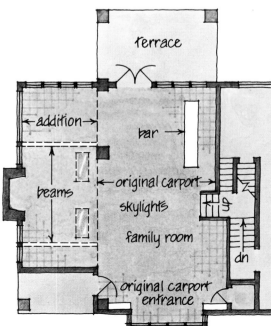

Their House Began with Rummaging

A Greensboro, North Carolina, couple started collecting with their first apartment and have not stopped since. The floors, ceiling beams, interior doors, and most furnishings in their family room came from drives down country roads.

A rustic country look seemed best suited to the building materials and collectibles this North Carolina family had accumulated after years of treasure hunting. The 12-inch-thick heart-pine beams in the family/dining area, for example, are from an old fertilizer plant and are 80 to 85 years old.

The flooring in the family room and throughout the house came from the Mount Hope Church in Guilford County and is approximately 100 years old. It was brushed clean, coated with urethane, and put down randomly in the new house. In some places, worn boards indicate where church aisles were once located.

"Just going to antique stores is no fun," says the father, who has spent a lifetime collecting everything from old lumber to antique blue-and-white enamelware. "You have to get out into the older, smaller towns—into barns, chicken houses, old dry-goods stores, onto front porches, under stairwells, in old woodsheds . . . If you do this, you can sometimes find treasures that you would never see in stores."

Above: A large open fireplace, with all the original features of a cooking fireplace, anchors one end of the family room. Antique cooking utensils, pots, and pans highlight the hearth.

Above, top: The family has furnished their entire house with a wide variety of antiques. Collections are displayed rather than stored.

Right: The combination family room, dining area, and kitchen, with exposed beams and flooring from an old church, has a warm ambience. The new interior walls were made from random-width, virgin-pine boards that were rough cut and stacked to dry. All interior walls were stained with a very light tint to achieve a weathered look, providing the perfect background for the antique furniture pieces and small collectibles scattered throughout the house.

122

They Subtracted a Wall, Multiplied the Use

Combining a former bedroom with the existing kitchen gave this New Orleans house a versatile family room. Now, kitchen and family room flow together with a relaxed, open feeling of space.

L ike many small houses built during the 1930s, this New Orleans cottage had no room large enough to serve as a family area. To solve the problem, the owners removed a wall between their kitchen and a small, unused bedroom at the rear of the house.

Where the wall once stood, a square table and chairs now provide a place for family dining. Angling the sofa into one corner and then placing chairs in corresponding positions provides an open place for children to play and a conversation area for five or six adults in the new sitting area.

Two large double-hung windows along the rear wall provide light and views to the rear garden. On one side, French doors lead to a new deck; above the doors, a paned transom adds more light. Floor-to-ceiling open bookshelves were added to frame the doors.

Above, right: The doorway leading from the hall was enlarged and made into a cased opening. Mexican tile covers the original vinyl flooring. The floor, finished with four to five coats of a special sealer, requires only an occasional damp mopping.

Left, above: Light floods the family room through the new double-hung windows and French doors with transom above.

Left: The breakfast table and chairs are where the bedroom wall used to be. The kitchen received a face-lift with new oak cabinets stained a rich, deep brown. The owners used a trim kit to cover appliances in a simulated wood grain to match the cabinets.

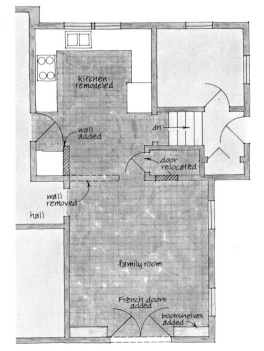

123

Above: Overall, the casual living area created from combining two rooms and adding a few feet gives the family a place to read and relax. Two skylights, two large windows on either side of the fireplace, and a paned door bring in light even on the cloudiest days.

Left: The formal living room next to the family area was also given new life. A large double-door opening between the two rooms now allows both areas to be used when entertaining. On either side of the opening, floor-to-ceiling bookcases fill the wall space, including the high, odd-shaped corner formed by the juncture of sloping roof and wall.

Right: This new family-room addition has an elevated, gently sloping ceiling above the fireplace. Adding a raised ceiling gives the room a distinctive character.

124

Added: Four Feet and Lots of Light

A family room addition, lighthearted in feeling and practical in use, provides space that is enjoyed by all. At one end, a raised ceiling with skylights gives the room a special lift.

Adding more family living space to their home helped meet the needs of a Birmingham couple who were already settled in a neighborhood that was too good to justify moving.

Combining two smaller rooms within existing walls would have created a casual family room, but the architect suggested a simple addition that resulted in distinctive character for this family room. A four-foot extension along one side wall included larger windows, a paned door, and two skylights in the raised, sloped ceiling of the addition. "Having a raised, sloping ceiling at the side of the room was really a response to matching a small sloped porch roof just beyond the new family room door," explains the architect. "In trying to get roof edges in order, the fireplace wall was added, about 4 feet past the end of the house."

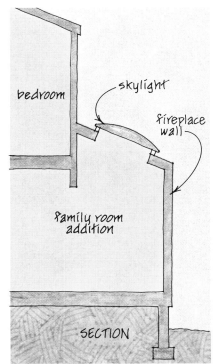

SECTION

A Light Touch for a Family Room

White walls and glass panels facing the trees brighten this paneled room. Light-filled and cheerful now, it is the hub of family activities day and night.

Family rooms are often dim, cavelike retreats that seem best suited for nighttime television viewing. But family rooms do not have to be dark. This family room in Raleigh, North Carolina, is meant to reflect the outside, and does just that. To maintain a feeling of outdoors, the room visually draws sunlight and trees into the space.

The V-groove paneling on three walls is painted white to reflect the natural light. You can repaint paneling without tedious stripping. Wipe small areas at a time with pre-paint liquid bonder (also called deglosser) and apply a primer coat when surface is tacky (30 to 60 minutes).

Above and right: The room maintains a feeling of outdoors with white-painted walls, a ceiling papered in a trellis pattern, and glass panels facing the trees.

Old Details, but a New Room

A new country-style family and dining room conversion proves that if you look hard enough, you can find clues to a delightful design even in the boxiest, most unfinished room in the house—the garage.

This new family/dining room in a Greenville, South Carolina, home contains little that is new. Yet the result is a startling transformation of a simple, coarse space into a warm, attractive room for entertaining and family living.

The not-so-obvious details make the remodeling work. The garage had three kinds of paneling—a board-and-batten wall, a V-grooved vertical plank wall, and a beaded-board ceiling. A piece of brick foundation showed through 7 inches at the base of all four walls. Instead of tearing them out or covering them up, the designer unified the background by simply painting all materials the same deep, bluish green. With as many as three textures in the woodwork and a fourth in the brick, the room took on a casual, rustic charm that would have been difficult to achieve with new materials.

Left: One wall was filled entirely with shelves for books and collections. Before the renovation, this window was the only one in the garage; others were added across the room.

Right: The family-room conversion, which enjoys a relaxed, rustic atmosphere, has space set aside for family dining.

Above, right: In the corner, the garage's existing board-and-batten and V-grooved paneling come together. These varying textures, united by a coat of bluish green paint, provide the basis for an eclectic room design that sets off the owners' collection of rustic memorabilia and antiques.

Above: One end wall sports an imaginative display of family treasures. A photograph of the wife's maternal great-grandparents, who were Tennessee farmers, is hung over a quilt made by the grandmother, bringing a rich tradition to the third generation's new room.

Right: Two pairs of French doors and a fireplace of old brick were built in where double garage doors used to be. Three windows were cut through a blank side wall. Decorative beams were added to the ceiling, and Mexican tiles were laid on the floor.

Living/Dining Rooms

They may be more formal than other rooms in the house. And individuality here tends to come from family antiques. But unique to living and dining rooms throughout the South is a friendliness, a relaxed formality that immediately puts a guest at ease.

Focus on the Fireplace Setting

A well-dressed fireplace can make a room. Come bask in the warmth of these.

The fireplace is usually the first thing you notice when you enter a room, and it is probably what you remember most when you leave. It is the focal point, the mood setter for a whole room. It should make an impact.

To accomplish this, consider the fireplace area as a unit. The separate components—walls, mantel area, furniture, and colors—should all work together.

COLOR sets the pace for the entire fireplace area. If you are painting the walls rather than using wallpaper or natural wood, do not be afraid to use vibrant, bold colors—deep blues, daffodil yellows, and mellow peaches. Cream or white semigloss or high-gloss paint (enamel is the most durable choice) on the mantel and surrounding woodwork will set them off against a dramatic wall color.

For darker colors, walls generally need at least two coats of paint to prevent spotting or streaking. Many dark colors look completely different when wet—they must be allowed to dry thoroughly before their true color shows.

THE AREA ABOVE THE FIREPLACE is a major focal point. Many people use only a painting or mirror on the chimney breast, but you might also want to add architectural detail like rich wooden paneling. Whatever you use should be large enough, and the image strong enough, to balance the size of the mantel and fireplace opening below.

ACCESSORIES for the mantel should be chosen to reinforce the overall feeling of the room and fireplace setting. Because the fireplace is architecturally symmetrical, it is best to keep the mantel accessories in balance as well by using a pair of objects. You can vary the pair, but try not to overweight one end of the mantel—keep a balanced feeling. This is known as a formal or symmetrical treatment. An informal or unmatched balance works well as long as the accessories on either end of the mantel have a common material or pattern.

Above: "We wanted the look of an old English parlor—the kind that has mahogany everywhere," say the owners of this living room. "But the cost would have been prohibitive, so we used a hint of paneling that tricks the eye to create a paneled-library look." Filling in the space between mantel and ceiling is a pickled birch panel with three raised sections. To create a cheery atmosphere year-round, a bright, rich yellow bathes the walls. The color is repeated in fabric and furnishings elsewhere in the room.

Far left: The built-ins flanking this fireplace give the living room the charm of an older house. The bookcases are capped with a shell niche that gives them a traditional appearance. Precast of high-density polyurethane, the shells are available in a variety of sizes and come primed in beige or white, ready to install. Once the shells are in place, they are trimmed with molding to match that used elsewhere in the room.

Professional designers are divided over whether a collection of small objects on the mantel is desirable. Some designers feel that a few important pieces, evenly balanced, make the only acceptable arrangement. Others like to display a collection on the mantel, where it is at eye level but out of reach of curious children.

If you want to use a collection of small objects, your arrangement should include a large painting, mirror, or wall hanging, centered on the wall, and a pair of dominant objects on either end of the mantel. These provide a core of balance for the smaller pieces. For the large central piece, choose something that will provide a neutral background, such as a graphic with little detail. Avoid using ornate frames and busy paintings that will compete with the collection.

BUILT-INS AND FURNITURE can be used on either side of the fireplace to frame the fireplace, adding to its architectural presence. Framing can be done either with built-ins or with furnishings.

If you do not use built-ins, furnishings can be arranged to highlight and draw attention to the fireplace. For example, you could frame the area with two end tables and a pair of lamps. The tables do not have to match, but they should be about the same size. If wall space does not permit using tables, chairs could be angled at either side of the fireplace.

Above, left: This fireplace area gets its lush feeling from the juniper green walls. The fireplace and paneled wainscoting, painted with white enamel, stand out in crisp contrast to the chimney breast. The owners used a large, antique English landscape painting to formalize the setting. A five-piece garniture across the mantel is in keeping with the formal painting. Pieces of mirror cover damaged marble surround, adding a touch of sparkle to the fireplace.

Left: In this casual-style living room, a nondescript surround was brought to life with hand-painted tiles. Painted in oranges and spring greens with a vine motif, the tiles center attention on the fireplace and away from the surrounding wall paneling. Since the mantel and wall area have no special architectural character, both were painted a creamy buttermilk color to provide a neutral backdrop for accessories. An antique English fender helps frame the lower edges of the firebox.

Right: Here, a collection of small objects creates an elegant display. A group of bud vases of varying heights and sizes marches across the mantel. Brass candlesticks with white tapers anchor either end. A mirror behind the vases makes a neutral backdrop, doubling the dramatic effect of the collection and also helping to add depth to the wide but shallow living area.

Furniture Makes an Informal Foyer

If there is no formal entry, you can arrange your furniture to create one.

When a young couple bought this Dallas house, they liked everything about it but the entry—or rather, the lack of one. To remedy this situation, they created their own foyer by arranging their furniture in two groupings, one on either side of the front door, making a corridor. This area now acts as a foyer—a welcoming spot for guests.

To emphasize the transition from outside to inside, a high chest anchors the wall opposite the door. It is the kind of piece often used in a foyer and helps make the visual connection.

The two seating areas are separate but not exclusive of one another. To keep an open feeling, none of the sofas are placed with their backs to the open space. And no high-backed chairs or large tables are located next to the foyer area.

Left: Plants are used throughout the room to soften corners and add height where needed. Windows are shuttered, adding to the room's uncluttered appearance.

Right, above: The entire grouping sits on a slight angle to the fireplace. The owners discovered this arrangement one Christmas when they needed a place for the tree. They put the two love seats facing each other but angling out from the wall on one side (see sketch). This created enough new space to the left of the fireplace for the tree. The grouping looked so good that the sofas were never moved back; a wing chair replaced the Christmas tree.

Right: The front door opens directly into this long, narrow living room. But an open area down the center of the room acts as a foyer. Enough space has been left between the sofa and the wall to form a passageway. The two groupings of furniture are not done in matching fabrics, but the colors—browns, tans, and roses—blend harmoniously.

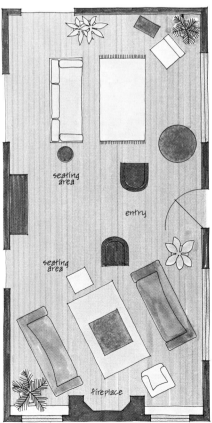

Old and New Create a Special Harmony

In this contemporary home design, the living and dining rooms are dramatic showcases for architectural antiques.

The wife in this family has been buying pieces of old buildings off and on for years. For maximum impact, however, the architectural antiques are used sparingly—only in the living and dining rooms. Some are integral parts of the new architecture, such as the columns which frame steps down into the dining area, creating a dramatic entrance. Other pieces in the living room are displayed as art, set within niches against a dark painted background. Furnishings are white and clean-lined to further spotlight the antiques.

Left and above: Architectural antiques warm and relax a contemporary living and dining room.

141

A Dining Room in the Center of Things

This plan for remodeling began with a need to improve circulation—both within the house and to the garden behind. A larger dining room was just one of the resulting benefits.

The new glass gallery adds only 5 feet to the back of the house. Even though it does not add much usable floor space, it stretches across three of the house's seven rooms, opening them up to garden views.

In the middle, where the dining room is now, the space is most open. The rear wall was completely removed, allowing room for the dining table to extend slightly into the gallery. The wall between the new dining room and living room was also removed and replaced with glass shelves flanking a cased opening. Light from the glass addition now streams through the center of the house.

Above: The gallery addition has a contemporary design, built of 4" x 6" cedar timbers with double glass both overhead and on its back wall. A Mexican tile floor sets the area apart from the original house, which has hardwood floors. The tiles also resist damage from the heavy traffic between the kitchen at one end and the bedroom at the other.

Far right: With the back wall of the house removed and the interior wall turned into a cased opening with glass shelves, the dining and living rooms are filled with light from the gallery. From the living room, the view is not of the addition itself, but rather of the dining room set against the garden beyond. The arrangement creates a formal symmetry, with the cased opening and open glass shelves framing the newly opened space.

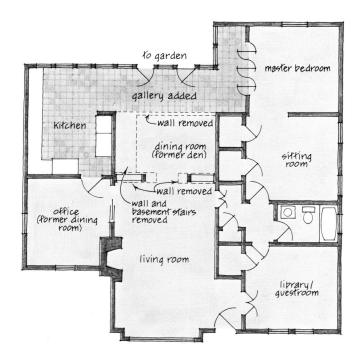

Sizing up a
Dining-Room Table

A dining room, used for entertaining, can be the most dramatic room in the house. It all centers around the table.

The dining room allows an adventurous spirit in decorating. Bold wall colors that you might be timid about in other rooms are suitable to the dining room because you will only spend a few hours there at a time while entertaining. And then you want to create a more dramatic and festive atmosphere for guests. Although you may want to coordinate colors between living and dining rooms that are open to one another, the dining room can often be treated as an independent room and handled in a singular, spectacular manner.

Even while surprising, the dining room is never far removed from tradition, however, through close association with holidays, family gatherings, and good friends. All of the rooms shown here represent ones found in homes across the South—each with an element of tradition but lightened with color, informal materials such as glass and rattan, or with an eclectic mix of contemporary furniture and antiques.

One thing is certain: Furniture counts for more in the dining room than in any other room in the house. Both the size and the style of the dining table and chairs set the tone for the entire room. Because it is such an important purchase, the dining table warrants more consideration than just an evaluation of the way it looks on the showroom floor. A few suggestions follow on size, shape, and materials to help you select a table that will suit your dining room and your style of entertaining.

Left: In a relatively small dining room, a glass-topped table provides maximum seating while visually expanding the room. A brass table base repeats the polished hardware of the antique Welsh cupboard and beautifully sets off the warm earth tones of the room. Simple shutters at the windows also make the room appear larger.

Left and above: The original handpainted wallpaper was considered a prize even though it had become dingy over the years. The homeowner carefully painted over the background, brightening the overall effect without losing the scenic mural. She also added touches of red to the neutral scenes, preserving the wallpaper while updating it to today's style.

Above: A glass-topped table and rattan chairs fit into this small dining room without seeming overbearing. The large china cabinet is also made less imposing by a light finish.

SIZE

Start out shopping with dining-room measurements in hand. In addition to the table size, there must be enough open space around the table for chairs to be pulled out for seating. About 4 feet on each side is ideal, and less than 3 feet would not be adequate.

SHAPE

Although the shape of the table should be chosen with the room dimensions in mind, your style of serving guests and family should be given equal consideration. If you have side pieces of furniture in the dining room, rectangular tables may appear to line up better, since all furniture lines will be parallel.

An oval table is a variation of the rectangular shape but looks lighter and actually does take up less floor space. Because corners take more space to walk around, rounded corners of any type leave more traffic space open. Therefore, oval or round tables seem to fit better in a smaller room. However, at the price of gaining more open space in the room, you lose surface space with an oval table.

A rectangular shape has the advantage of slightly more outside seating as well as more center space for serving dishes. The decision between oval and rectangular could depend on whether you enjoy serving from a buffet or prefer to serve all food on the table.

While a large, square dining table has important impact in a room, there is a problem of inflexible seating. How do you intimately seat four people at a large square table? A square table can get so large that reaching another person presents serving difficulties, too. A smaller square table does not present these problems, but it is more suitable for casual meals.

There is something magically convivial about a round table, which tends to spark conversation—perhaps it is because there is no head of the table and seating is less formal. If your room will accommodate a round table larger than 42 to 54 inches in diameter, however, you may have to find an antique. Most round tables manufactured today are 36 to 42 inches wide; leaves extend them to oval shapes.

Ideally a guest can be seated every 2 feet around any table, but leg spacing beneath the table can limit the crowd. Pedestals and corner legs do not interfere with seating, but poorly spaced legs on an oval table can eliminate an extra place setting on each side of the table. Although they are convenient in tight, dual-purpose rooms, the legs of drop-leaf tables are almost always in the way of seating, leaving room for only one person in the center section.

146

Above: The pedestal base of this contemporary wooden table eliminates the chance of a guest straddling a table leg, but has the disadvantage of not being expandable for larger dinner parties. Though sleek in style, the thick wooden tabletop beautifully complements antique Chippendale chairs, richly upholstered in burgundy suede.

MATERIALS

Glass-top tables tend to make a room appear larger, so glass is a good solution in very small rooms or over a spectacular rug. They have the disadvantage of not being expandable.

If you prefer wood, you still have a choice between light and dark finishes and textured effects. Dark wood finishes have a richer tone and are generally more formal. But a light finish might be just the boost you need in a dark room with little natural light. Light wood can also be dramatic against a wooden floor, where a dark table on a dark floor would seem too heavy.

The relation of textures in a room is important to the warmth and comfortable feel of the room, and the grain of a wooden table becomes another texture in the room just like the wall covering or carpet.

Herringbone and parquet patterns on dining tables can bring in desirable textures, but they require coordination with other textures in the room. For example, a room with a parquet floor does not really need strong texture in the table. The texture of a table must also work with your table appointments; delicate china will look awkward on a highly textured table.

Garden Rooms

Once essential to comfortable summer living in the South, garden rooms are now part of the family's year-round living space. Garden room, sunroom, porch, or greenhouse—all open the house to natural light and garden views.

One New Room Can Brighten the Whole House

This added living space, formerly a back porch, has lots of personality. Natural light and garden views now penetrate the house.

T he house had always been dark," explain the owners of this home in Tulsa. "By removing a rear wall and enclosing the back porch with lots of glass, we were able to lighten the kitchen, dining, and living rooms."

To achieve maximum natural light, their architect wrapped the rear wall of the new sunroom with three large windows and a pair of French doors. In addition, three skylights punctuate the space between beams in the new vaulted ceiling. Together, windows and skylights bring an abundance of light into the room. The adjoining living room, dining room, and kitchen all benefit from the exposure.

Before remodeling, the family room could only be reached by passing through the living room. By relocating the door opening from the living room to one end of the new sunroom, traffic now can circumvent the living area.

Right and above right: This 10- x 15-foot space, once a porch at the rear of a 1950s house, is now a light-filled room with many uses. The original brick floor was kept for easy maintenance in a high-traffic and plant display area and for its heat-retaining properties. A new vaulted ceiling, framed by wide beams, seems to double the space. The abundance of sunlight makes the space ideal for indoor plants. Adjoining interior rooms benefit from natural light admitted by the large windows, French doors, and skylights. In summer, large deciduous trees near the rear of the house help shade the room from direct heat. The large insulated-glass windows have snap-in wooden muntins for easy cleaning.

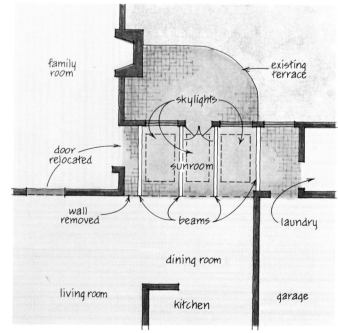

A New Day for the Sunroom

Whether you call them sunrooms or garden rooms, they make good energy sense for the South, given the right exposure. And as these examples show, they can invite all-season living, too.

Once considered an essential for a well-designed Southern home, the sunroom is being rediscovered by people throughout the South. Many homeowners are enclosing porches, expanding garden rooms, building new sunrooms, or simply making better use of the sunrooms they already have.

Besides gaining an attractive, versatile space that is usable year-round for entertaining and family activities, there are other practical benefits of sunrooms. A properly designed, oriented, and insulated sunroom serves as a source of natural light; it also collects the sun's heat, which helps warm a house, supplementing gas or electric heat.

Sunrooms have been decorated traditionally in white wicker or with wrought-iron furniture. Today, they are taking on a new elegance and visual appeal, furnished with an imaginative selection of furniture, artwork, accessories, even antiques. There is a sense of freedom in the use of color, even a spirit of playfulness in the treatment of traditional features, such as latticework, skylights, and painted floors.

DESIGNING A SUNROOM

It is a good idea to consult an architect when planning to build a sunroom or make any structural changes in an existing area of your house. While designing a room to serve the functions you have in mind, an architect will also help you achieve the quality of natural light you desire and obtain the greatest benefit from available solar energy.

For example, if your site has sufficient privacy and several well-placed deciduous shade trees, your architect will probably encourage you to make use of solar energy by placing a number of

Left and above: Enclosing a long, narrow porch with thermal glass created this sunny, spacious garden room. Skylights positioned above interior doorways help brighten the rooms adjoining the porch. Brick flooring is ideal for absorbing heat during the day and releasing it at night to help warm the adjoining rooms.

windows on the south side of the house. Such a room will receive good morning light and also serve as a passive collector of solar heat. Proper-size deciduous trees, fast-growing deciduous vines, and well-located roof overhangs and canvas awnings will shade the interior from the sun's direct rays in summer, preventing excessive heat gain. In winter, when the trees and vines have lost their leaves and the sun is lower in the sky, the sun's rays will penetrate the house's interior and warm surfaces there.

Above: An antique settee, wing chair, and other fine pieces used in this sunroom continue the decorative theme established in the traditionally furnished home. When furnishing a sunroom, it is a good idea to use light-colored fabrics to lessen the chances of their fading.

Right: This curved addition to an existing room not only created a large, bright sunroom but also provided a flow between the kitchen and family room. Pie-shaped segments of glass fitted between ceiling joists created a distinctive light source at the top of the addition. One traditional sunroom feature, the painted floor, received a unique treatment here. The floor was painted dark green; the artist then added this flowing pattern of birds and magnolia blossoms. Note how the simplicity of the furnishings adds to the open, airy feeling.

Windows and Ventilation

Double-glazed, reflective, and thermal glass windows are available for insulating a glass-enclosed room from extreme outside temperatures. Double-glazed windows have up to an inch of airspace between two pieces of glass to act as insulation. Reflective glass is specially coated to repel the sun's heat when direct solar gain is not desired. Thermal glass has a thin insulating air pocket between the sheets of glass. (One method of cutting the high cost of large expanses of thermal glass is to design the window openings to accommodate standard-size replacement panels made for sliding glass doors.)

It is important to provide natural ventilation in a sunroom so the room will be comfortable without air conditioning. In summer, ceiling fans are useful for generating a breeze inside the room; in winter, a fan will help recirculate warm air collecting at the ceiling.

Skylights

Skylights give a solariumlike effect to a dark area. One or more skylights can be positioned to brighten the center of a room, illuminate an architectural feature, or wash a wall.

Furnishing a Sunroom

Many interior designers suggest limiting the amount of furniture placed in a sunroom that is designed to be open and airy. Let one table, such as a square table for four, serve both as a dining table and game table.

Furniture in the garden room can complement the furniture styles found in other rooms of the house, or project a different style, depending upon the effect desired. Antique settees and oak chairs, contemporary wicker sofas and ottomans, or a mixture of both styles can be used. Fabrics should be light colored in a room that receives a lot of sun to lessen the chance of their fading.

Shutters, shades, rattan and matchstick blinds, even folding screens used at the windows aid in sun control. Thin-slatted aluminum blinds are also a good choice for sunrooms, because they are completely adjustable for light control and available in many colors. Avoid choosing dark-colored fabrics for window treatments, as they tend to fade.

Lighting can focus attention on a particular area within a room. Placing banks of downlights on rheostats will help you achieve a particularly wide variety of effects. Well-located exterior lighting will make outside plantings a feature of your sunroom and give it an illusion of greater depth at night. Install all exterior lights with dimmers for the greatest range of effects.

Island Living in White and Wicker

Refreshing openness and a spirited mix of furnishings in this home make it a true expression of its setting.

Cool white tiles and white fabrics are especially well-suited to sun-filled spaces in this Hilton Head Island home. When working with a neutral color scheme, however, great variety is needed in both furnishings and textures to keep a room interesting. The owner of this island home has blended her favorite antiques with wicker furniture, lots of baskets, and plants; this avoids a heavy or formal look, which would seem confining in an island home.

The vertical emphasis and overscaled openness of the architecture help to complement the clean, cool look of white furnishings. A 12-foot-square skylight in the center of the living room is supported by a double-hip roof, and four salvaged columns emphasize the skylight's loft.

With large, spacious rooms organized in a U shape around a pool and terrace in the back, the house manages to be very open to light and views but retains maximum privacy. All walls facing the pool are glass or sliding-glass doors, which open up the whole house to a view of the pool and the lagoon beyond. But the outside walls maintain privacy by containing small windows or none at all.

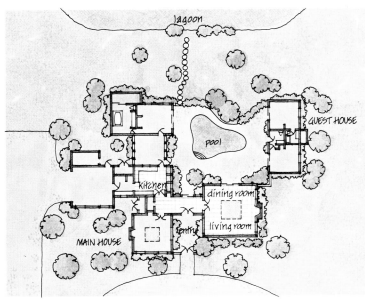

Above, left: Natural wicker love seats and two white wing chairs are skillfully combined with a glass-top cocktail table to form the major seating group in the living room. The long-shag carpet provides a contrast of textures with a slick tile floor. A large skylight emphasizes the openness of the room and allows lush plant growth.

Right: Greenhouse construction extends the kitchen into a delightful breakfast area that features white wicker seating. Cool white tile runs throughout the kitchen and foyer.

Planning Your Greenhouse

In recent years, greenhouses have added new functions to their traditional role as a place for plants. Now they are also places for people, and they are devices for catching the sun's warmth to save on home-heating costs.

Whether you plan a greenhouse just for living space or for a combination of uses, there can be a comfortable balance between a greenhouse that is suitable for plants or energy and one that is comfortable for people. But before you begin, set your priorities. Exactly which functions—or combination of functions—are most important to you?

Here are some facts you should consider before you remodel or build.

ORIENTATION

A greenhouse with any southern exposure at all will aid in solar heat gain, though the more southerly the exposure, the more efficient the gain. For simple livability or for plants, the best orientation is southeastern. This gives some southern exposure, but not during the hottest part of the day. Southern or eastern exposures are next in preference. The last choice would be a western exposure, where the afternoon sun can make a greenhouse too hot, or a northern one, where there may be insufficient sunlight for many types of plants.

Obstructions

When planning your greenhouse, observe the movement of the sun and shade, especially if you intend to use your greenhouse for solar heat gain. A neighbor's house or evergreen trees may

Left: Tile flooring and oak table and chairs transformed an existing, detached greenhouse into a greenhouse dining room with warm good looks. To make room for entertaining, the owners removed the center bench. A pebble border under the two side benches allows free drainage.

block too much sun for the greenhouse to be effective. But deciduous trees are better than no trees at all. In the winter, they let light and warmth into the greenhouse when you need it most. In the summer, they shade the greenhouse and keep it from becoming too hot.

CONNECTION WITH THE HOUSE
Especially for greenhouses used as living spaces, large openings can bring the outdoor atmosphere of a greenhouse into the main house. If you want to maintain a true greenhouse atmosphere, sliding-glass doors or French doors may be added to close the opening. Either way, the glass doors retain views to the greenhouse.

If you have the proper orientation and a place to connect a greenhouse to your home, you next must decide whether to build a lean-to or a pitched-roof greenhouse that attaches to the house at its gable end.

The Lean-To
This generally is the least expensive type of greenhouse to build, because its connection to the house eliminates large areas of glass. It also is the most efficient for solar gain because the decreased glass area reduces surfaces that lose heat at night, and because its shape, with the long side against the house, absorbs the sun's heat best.

Pitched-Roof
The more complicated structure and increased glass area on this shape make it more expensive than a lean-to. Because of the increased amount of glass and because it attaches to the house with its short gable end, it loses more heat at night and gains more in the day than does a lean-to. Its smaller connection to the house makes moving the warm air into the main living space more difficult. However, a pitched-roof greenhouse offers better sunlight for plants. And it can be a very pleasant place for people. Because it projects farther from the house than a lean-to, it can give the feeling of a pavilion in the yard.

CUSTOM DESIGN OR PREFABRICATED
Once you decide on the configuration of your greenhouse, you need to decide whether to buy or build. You can custom design and build your greenhouse, or you can buy one of the many prefabricated ones that have come onto the market in recent years.

Custom Design
This is particularly advantageous if you are going to use your greenhouse to aid in heating your home. You can design the slope of the glass walls so they are most efficient for catching the sun in your latitude. Similarly, you can design the roof pitch to minimize summer heat gain. If

Above: This custom, pitched-roof greenhouse is a well-scaled addition to a charming Victorian house in Knoxville, Tennessee. The owners invite friends for elegant dinners there, icing the wine down in a sink in the potting bench.

Far left: The large lean-to greenhouse provides a year-round place for plants and people. A rollup awning (not shown) is used for sun control on the south-facing structure.

you have a solid rather than a glass roof, you can design overhangs so they shade the glass walls in summer. You can select the materials you wish, using, for example, acrylic sheeting instead of glass to save money. (Here, you must again consider your priorities. Acrylic may not be sufficiently transparent for a pleasant living space, but it may be adequate for a greenhouse used for heat gain or growing plants.) Another choice you have with custom design is the framing material. A custom greenhouse probably will be framed of wood because it is easier to work. Wood has another advantage: It does not transmit heat as quickly as metal from a warm inside to a cold outside, so heat loss at night is less. However, wood does require painting and other maintenance.

Prefabricated

These come in a variety of shapes and heights in both lean-to and pitched-roof shapes. They are modular so their length can be extended simply by adding more of their identical glass sections. Height can vary from those only slightly taller than the greenhouse door to those that extend two stories. They are available both in models that are installed directly on a concrete slab (in which the glass extends to the ground) and in those that are built on a base wall around a slab's perimeter. They also may be installed as an integral part of the house, as a large bay window or on a balcony, for example.

TEMPERATURE AND SUN CONTROL

Tinted glass usually is available, as is double- and triple-pane glass, which cut down on both heat gain and heat loss. Some systems of frosted fiberglass keep out direct sunlight and diffuse light through the interior space. Other greenhouses offer shades and blinds designed to fit their windows. Whichever you choose, you almost certainly will want some kind of sun control to keep the greenhouse from becoming too warm and to keep the bright sunlight from fading furniture fabrics. If your main concern is solar heat gain, or if you have no doors to close off the greenhouse from the rest of the house at night, you also will likely want to install window quilts or some other form of heavy shade to cut down on heat loss at night. A greenhouse built for heat gain also may have a fan (possibly controlled by a thermostat) to move the warm air from the greenhouse into the main house by day. But if openings to the house are positioned correctly at the bottom of the wall, to draw cold air into the greenhouse and, at the top, to send the warmed air back, natural air currents may eliminate the need for a fan.

Above: An extension to a family room, this custom-built, wood-framed greenhouse construction opens up the room to a wooded area behind the house. Wicker and rattan furniture and a sisal rug are in keeping with the indoor/outdoor feeling, and the neutral fabric colors are less likely to fade in the strong sunlight.

Above: A lean-to greenhouse was used instead of conventional dry wall construction for the end wall of this family room. The greenhouse, planned more for people than for plant growth, brightens the interiors and opens the room to a view of a swimming pool and a valley overlook beyond.

FLOORS

Greenhouses for living space usually substitute brick or tile for the pebble floors of greenhouses that are for plants. In a greenhouse designed for both plants and people, the brick or tile may be sloped toward a center drain so it can be hosed down; pebbles also may be used around the perimeter, under plant benches. A solar greenhouse should have a dark masonry flooring of brick, tile, concrete, or stone to make sure that heat is absorbed by day and radiated back at night.

MOISTURE

If you are not using your greenhouse primarily for plants, moisture will not be too great a problem. But most greenhouses have some condensation on the glass, especially on the roof, so they usually come equipped with a system of gutters to carry off moisture. If a greenhouse maintains a high humidity for plants and is also used for living, choose your furnishings carefully. One option is to move your furnishings in only temporarily while you are using the greenhouse; another is to select furnishings carefully.

What a Porch!

Two stories tall and wrapped with screen, this porch addition combines the best of indoor and outdoor living.

You do not need to convince most Southerners of the advantages of the screen porch. It has been a necessary piece of survival gear for many years, keeping insects out and letting breezes through. In today's air-conditioned world, the screened porch is still a favorite place to be.

But few screened porches approach the scope and scale of this addition to an Austin, Texas, home. Measuring 18 x 24 feet and reaching 25 feet high, the porch serves as an outdoor living space. Translucent fiberglass on the roof creates a play of light and shadow that reinforces the feeling of being outside. Shaded by nearby trees, open to the breeze on three sides, and equipped with a ceiling fan, the porch stays pleasant even on hot days.

Above and right: The porch was designed to complement the steeply pitched roofline and high gable ends of the existing house. But to keep the massive screened porch from overpowering the house, the architect used the lightest possible framing material. One bonus of the light construction is the reduced cost, which is about one-third of a conventional, glassed-in addition.

Living with the Environment

Whether it means saving the trees on a wooded suburban lot, orienting the house for sun and breeze, or building a vacation home on the water, living with the environment is the goal of many Southern homeowners. Though the terminology of land and energy conservation is new, the indigenous design principles and a traditional respect for the land go back three hundred years.

Designing with the Environment is Nothing New

Look at what your ancestors did to keep their homes warm or cool; it can work cost efficiently for you, too.

Above: Oakley, a Louisiana raised cottage, is a product of the warm, damp bayou climate. Elevated anywhere from a few feet to a full story above the ground, the raised cottage takes advantage of breezes and avoids ground dampness and flooding. Broad roof overhangs create shady galleries and porches for outdoor living.

Above, top: Charleston settlers turned their homes at a right angle to the street to catch cooling breezes. Broad galleries at the Edmonston-Alston house shade outdoor living areas and help cool air before it enters the house. High ceilings help lift hot air up and out of the way.

Rising costs and an awareness of shrinking energy supplies have forced many Southern homeowners to look again at the techniques our ancestors used to stay comfortable in Southern climates. These techniques resulted in indigenous architectural styles you can adapt to your own home for energy-saving comfort.

Charleston Single House—Blessed with mild winters but cursed with hot, muggy summers, the builders of colonial Charleston placed their main emphasis on keeping cool. By turning their houses at a right angle to the street, they could take advantage of cooling breezes from the water (and also save on property taxes, which were based on front footage).

Broad galleries along the side of a Charleston-style house provide a shaded outdoor living area and also help to cool the air before it enters the house. Since the houses are only one room wide (hence the name single house), cross ventilation is very efficient. High ceilings help keep the hot air up and away from the occupants.

Monticello—Passive cooling techniques are as much a part of Thomas Jefferson's home near Charlottesville, Virginia, as the dumbwaiter and Palladian architecture. Built on a hilltop, the plantation house takes maximum advantage of the prevailing winds.

Large windows open the house to the breezes, while covered porches help precool the air entering the house. The flanking dependencies are nestled into the hillside to minimize their visual impact, and at the same time provide the earth-cooling effect of an underground structure. Arcades linking the dependencies with the main house also provide a shaded, cooler path for air entering the house. There is even a strong suspicion that the skylights and stairways serve as

Above: Thomas Jefferson's Monticello, his plantation home near Charlottesville, Virginia, takes full advantage of the prevailing winds at its hilltop site. The house uses large windows, covered porches, and arcades to catch and precool breezes.

thermal chimneys to help exhaust hot air from the house. The massive brick exterior walls also serve as thermal storage walls, slowing the transmission of heat from the outside during the day so that it reaches the interior during the evening.

Louisiana Raised Cottage—The flat, damp bayou country presented its early settlers with a challenging climate. They rose above it, literally, by developing the raised cottage. Elevated anywhere from a few feet to a full story above the ground, the raised cottage takes advantage of cooling breezes while avoiding the dampness of the ground and occasional flooding.

Broad roof overhangs provide shade during the summer and create galleries and porches (sometimes screened for outdoor living). Full floor-to-ceiling windows open the house for natural ventilation, and high ceilings inside help in summer cooling.

West Texas Adobe House—The hot, arid climate of West Texas features very hot days and cool nights—climatic conditions that allow the building structure itself to be used for cooling during the day and for warmth at night. Using this day-to-night temperature swing and a local building material—adobe—to the best advantage, houses with massive walls were developed. The thick adobe walls slow the conduction of heat from the outside during the day. As the walls gradually warm from the sun, they slowly begin to transmit heat to the inside. With the proper wall thickness, the sun's heat is blocked out during the day, and then, during the cooler night, the stored heat is gradually released to the interior of the house. (See following story.)

West Texas Oasis

Walled away from the hot, dry days of West Texas, this Midland residence creates its own special space inside. Both in concept and plan, it is much like the original mission architecture which developed in response to the desertlike climate of the Southwest.

Flat and semiarid, the plains of West Texas are not the most hospitable. So rather than open this contemporary house outward to its surroundings, the architect/owner turned the house in on itself. By building a wall, and then a house behind the wall, a new space—more amiable, more hospitable—is created (*see section drawing*). It is far easier to deal with than the limitless horizons of the surrounding prairie landscape. The wall also helps to cut the effect of the winter wind. Overall, the house is very urban, a private place closed off from its surroundings.

The heart of the house is the 24-foot-square living area. Clustered around this central space—pinwheel fashion—are a dining alcove, the bedrooms, a library, and the kitchen. Because of the privacy afforded by the walled lot, there was greater flexibility in the placement of the rooms of the house relative to the site. For example, the bedrooms are located at what

Above: From the street, only the galvanized iron roof of the house is visible over the cedar wall that surrounds the site. Rectangular skylights bring natural light into the living area.

Right: Measuring 24 feet square and almost 30 feet high, the living area is a light, airy, open space at the heart of the house. Exposed wooden roof trusses also support track lights.

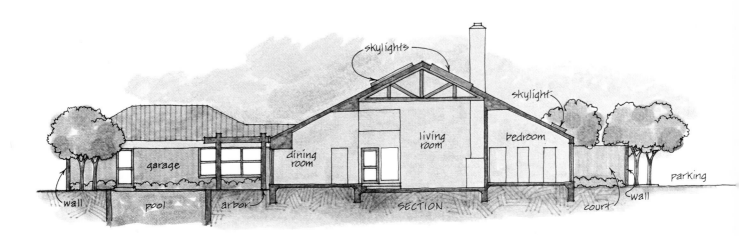

would normally be the front of the house, closest to the street. Separated as they are by the privacy wall and a 10-foot-wide courtyard, the bedrooms are most secluded. The wall also allows the bedrooms to be located on the east side of the house, a position that makes them cooler on summer nights than a location on the west side of the house, where they could be heated by the afternoon sun.

Above: Lighted by a large skylight, the 4- x 7-foot kitchen island provides plenty of work space.

Above, right: The dining room is in an alcove off the main living space. Bedrooms, a library, and the kitchen are also clustered—pinwheel fashion—around the central living space. Floors throughout the house are Mexican tile laid on the diagonal.

Left: An arbor shades the narrow terrace between the pool and house; a roll-down canvas awning provides extra screening from the low afternoon sun.

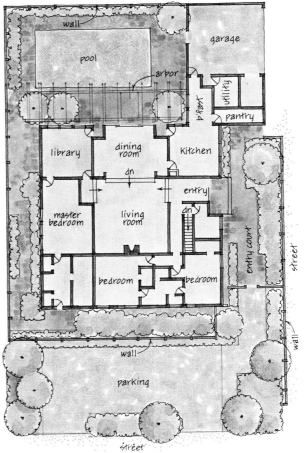

173

Cooling with Tradition in Tampa

Native architectural forms help this new Florida house ventilate itself. Both plan and detailing have an old-fashioned simplicity.

Above: Windows in the cupola, which rises 30 feet above the floor, are opened with a log pole of the type used by power companies to cut off transformers. The windows are hinged at the bottom and are sheltered by a roof overhang above, so that even blowing rain does not come in. The cupola draws so well that strong breezes slam the windows shut by themselves—a noisy, but certainly convenient, happenstance.

Far right: The plan of the house is as simple as its cooling techniques. The house is 45 feet square, with a dogtrot room in the center. Building codes required the house to be 11 feet above sea level to protect it from occasional high water in the tidal estuary which borders one side of the lot. But the architect made sure the open section below had enough headroom (the house wound up 7 feet 10 inches above grade) so the space underneath was usable. It now serves for parking and storage and doubles as a recreation area. The extra height also means that the house receives generous breezes.

This Tampa home offers a sample of Florida history. The lush site overhung with palms and live oaks recalls a time when the state had been touched by few people. The wood construction and steep metal roof recall native forms of Florida architecture, too. But the house blends the present with the past. For while the state's landscape has changed with a growing population, the old-fashioned concerns of a tropical environment remain concerns today—particularly the need to keep cool in the summertime.

Traditional Florida houses often were built in two sections with a porch called a dogtrot between them. This allowed cooling breezes to flow around and through as many rooms as possible. Another technique was to build a cupola atop the roof peak. When windows in both cupola and house were opened, warm air rose up and out, and the cooler outside air was drawn in below.

This Tampa home combines the two methods of cooling. The dogtrot was enclosed for the kitchen, living, and dining areas. But the enclosures are sliding-glass doors that allow generous airflow for ventilation through a cupola.

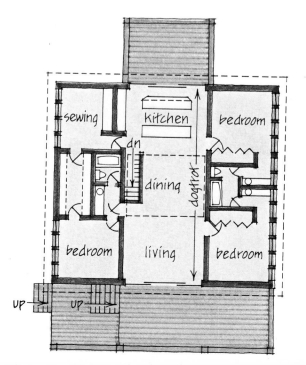

Heated and Cooled by Sun and Wind

Warm in winter, cool in summer, this house uses the sun and the wind to keep it comfortable year-round. The key to the simple passive system is a three-story greenhouse that acts as a solar collector.

One of the best ways to heat a house is to place windows on the south side of the structure and simply let the sun shine in. This site in Midlothian, Virginia, has the privacy, natural tree cover, and southerly orientation that enabled the owners to build a house heated primarily by direct-gain solar energy. Breezes cool the structure naturally in summer.

The home's system of passive solar heating requires no special equipment to utilize the sun's rays. Casement windows, a greenhouse, a whole-house fan, and ceiling and exhaust fans control the temperature and circulation of air. A heat pump is always available for backup use.

This commonsense plan, substituting sunlight and air currents for expensive fuel, has proven quite effective. The owner explains, "We moved from a smaller house in the same neighborhood where our electric bills were several hundred dollars a month. This house has over 3,000 square feet and is totally electric. Our electric bills range from approximately $40 to a high one month of around $100." Lighting costs are also lower since the owners seldom have to turn on a lamp during the day, thanks to the abundance of natural light.

Above: Located next to the kitchen, the family room contains a small greenhouse breakfast area. The sliding-glass doors open to a screened porch.

Left: At the rear, a three-story-high greenhouse, custom-made from stock components, traps solar heat. A sliding-glass door at the base of the greenhouse opens to release warm air into the house. A tile floor also helps store the sun's heat in winter. In summer, casement windows swing open to catch the lake breezes and an exhaust fan in the greenhouse roof vents excess heat.

177

WINTER HEATING

The windowless north side of the cedar-shingled house gives privacy at the street and protection from northern winds. The presence of large beech trees on the south side of the property and its orientation overlooking a lake made it possible to install many windows at the rear of the house without loss of privacy. Insulated casement windows and a greenhouse admit sunlight to the house while opening the structure to panoramic views of the lake.

In winter, when the sun is at a low angle and trees drop their leaves, sunlight enters the glassed areas and heats the interior surfaces. Heat absorbed in the daytime radiates into the house at night.

SUMMER COOLING

When warm weather arrives, the trees between the house and lake have regained their leaves and shade the windows quite effectively. The owners say, "We were afraid that the cost of cooling the house would offset the savings in winter. But the lot is so heavily wooded that the house is completely shaded. We sit on the hill and get all the cool breezes from the lake."

The ceiling fans and the whole-house fans keep the air flowing. The exhaust fan in the greenhouse provides additional ventilation needed to keep this indoor-outdoor living space comfortable.

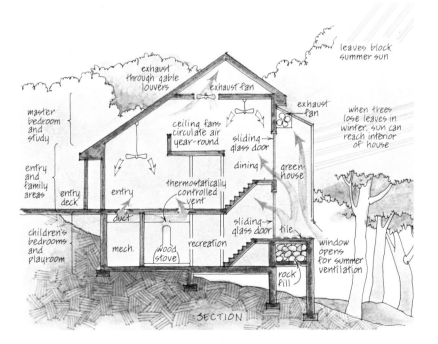

Right: On the street side, cedar siding closes off the front of the house for privacy and blocks northerly winds in the winter. The entry level is the middle floor of the three-story house.

Climate-Responsive Houses

Passive solar design can put your home in tune with the environment. The results can be both interesting architecture and greatly reduced power bills.

There are two basic ways you can achieve a comfortable environment in your house: the active method of using energy to mechanically heat or cool the space, or the more subtle passive method of home design that uses the forces of nature to create the desired comfort level. The latter is also called passive solar design, and it is really a combination of common-sense design and adaptation of regional styles that were developed before the widespread use of mechanical heating and cooling. The basic principle of passive solar design is to use the sun to heat the house in winter and to keep the hot sun out of the house in summer.

Because of the sun's lower altitude in the winter months, this can easily be achieved by orienting the house to the south and opening the maximum amount of glass to the lower winter rays. In summer the sun is higher, and roof overhangs can block the sun's rays from the interior of the house.

PASSIVE SOLAR HOME DESIGN

Simple in concept and operation and costing little more than conventional design, the direct-gain passive solar concept can offer considerable energy savings when compared to mechanical heating and cooling systems. Savings of a third to a half on winter utility bills are often reported by the owners of the simple, direct-gain-system houses.

Natural cooling in warm weather is, in many ways, a harder goal to achieve than passive solar heating. Two of the oldest cooling techniques are still among the best: deep roof overhangs for shading from the sun and operable windows for natural ventilation.

One problem frequently encountered with passive-cooled houses is high humidity. In addition to the discomfort, there can be problems with mildew, especially in closets or other areas of low air movement. Humidity can be reduced mechanically by a dehumidifier or an air conditioner. Alternatively, the uncomfortable, sticky feeling can be lessened by increasing the air flow through the house.

Using fans throughout the house is one way to augment the natural ventilation. Another method is the thermal chimney (also called solar chimney). The thermal chimney works much like an ordinary chimney to produce a draft that draws warm air out of the house and encourages natural ventilation. The thermal chimney uses heat from the sun to create the draft.

There are many approaches to the problems of passive solar home design. In fact, most houses use a combination of systems. If you interested in building a passive solar house, first study the various systems available, remembering that there are different ways to approach each problem. Then find an architect or engineer with experience in the design of passive solar houses. Most state solar energy organizations can supply a list of designers interested in doing passive solar homes.

A newer method still being proven is to use the lower temperature of the earth to pre-cool air before it enters the house. Basically, this earth-cooling system consists of tubes buried in the earth with one end open to the outside air, the other end opening into the house. Outside air passes through the tubes on its way into the house and is cooled down to the approximate ground temperature (70 to 75 degrees in the Middle South during the summer) before entering the house. The earth-cooling system does all the work, although data is incomplete on the many variables that affect the efficiency of the system, such as size, length, and material of the cooling tubes and the depth of the installation.

What about Active Solar Energy?

In determining the wisdom of an active solar heating system, the jury is still out. Still, some Southern homeowners are voting for their long-range payoff.

Unlike the various passive systems that use the whole house to gather the sun's warmth, active systems utilize collectors (usually flat-plate types mounted on the roof) to catch the solar radiation. This heat is then pumped through a more or less conventional system to heat the house. Similar solar collectors are used for domestic water heating.

All active solar collectors on the market work in much the same way. The flat-plate collector usually consists of a black-painted copper or aluminum panel containing tubes through which a liquid flows (either water or a water-antifreeze mixture). The collector panel is covered with glass or plastic that will allow the solar radiation in, warming the panels, but will minimize heat loss back to the outside air.

The number of collector panels needed to heat a house will depend on the size of the house, the average sunlight falling in the area, tree coverage, and orientation of the house. Typically, collectors equal to about a third of the total square footage of the house are needed for whole-house solar heating. For hot water, only 40 to 80 square feet of collectors are needed.

The collectors absorb radiant energy from the sun, heating the liquid in the tubes. The heated liquid is pumped to a heat exchanger, where it warms the air in a forced-air heating system. Other systems circulate heated water through baseboard radiators to warm the house. For domestic hot water, the heat exchanger is usually placed in the hot-water tank, where tap water is heated for washing and bathing.

To allow for overcast days and nights, most active solar systems include a heat storage system, usually a very large tank of water, which can store heat for days. Hot-air systems use containers filled with rocks for storage.

IS IT COST EFFECTIVE?

While active solar systems are effective, both for whole-house heating and for domestic hot water, one significant factor limiting widespread use is their high initial cost. Typical installation costs range from $7,000 to $10,000 or more for a whole-house system (versus about $2,000 to $2,500 for a conventional heating and air-conditioning system). Solar hot-water heating systems range from $1,000 to $2,500 or more, whereas a gas or electric hot-water heater costs only a few hundred dollars.

The amount of energy savings from using a solar heating or hot-water system will depend on many factors, including actual solar radiation, number of cloudy days, winter temperatures, and, most important of all, cost of conventional fuel. Generally, however, a solar heating or domestic hot-water system should be expected to cut fuel consumption by 50 percent or more when compared with a conventional gas or electric system. Conventional energy sources are still needed for standby use when there is insufficient sunlight or when stored heat is unavailable.

Since utility rates vary greatly across the South, it is difficult to make any broad statements about the cost-effectiveness of active solar systems compared to conventionally fueled systems. However, active solar heating is usually considered to be an economically viable alternative to electric resistance heating and to electric hot-water heaters.

On the other hand, the low installation cost and relatively low price of natural gas as well as the high efficiency of heat pumps makes them more economical, at this time, than an active solar system. However, if utility rates rise considerably, the situation could reverse and the active solar systems would be more economical.

Landscaping for Energy Conservation

Perhaps the single most effective means of reducing those costs lies outside in your garden.

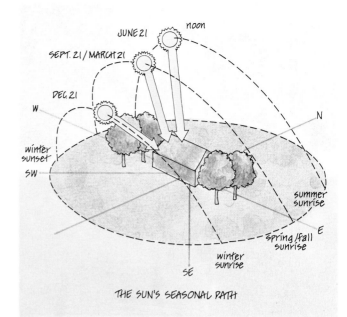

THE SUN'S SEASONAL PATH

When plants—especially trees and vines—are strategically placed, they can significantly reduce your home's energy consumption. By using the landscaping approach to energy conservation, you not only can reduce the energy burden on your indoor heating and cooling systems, but you can enhance the livability of your outdoor environment at the same time.

Here are a few tips on providing shade in summer and protection from winds in winter.

SHADING WITH TREES

Shading a house can reduce the indoor temperature by as much as 10 degrees. This means a decreased burden on air conditioning, which results in a savings of both energy and money.

The placement of shade trees, of course, depends on the sun's path across the sky, which changes with the seasons. In summer, it sweeps the sky in a long arc that begins low in the east at dawn, climbing higher until it is nearly overhead at midday, then sinks to the west at sunset. In winter, the arc is much shorter and lower in the sky, rising in the southeast and setting in the southwest.

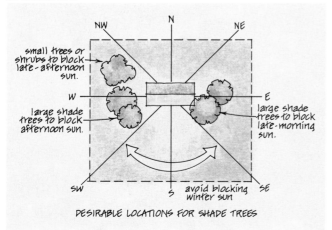

DESIRABLE LOCATIONS FOR SHADE TREES

The objective of planting shade trees is to block intense summer sun from your home and terrace while allowing winter sun to provide needed warmth. Generally, deciduous trees are best for serving both needs. (For those best suited to your area, consult your local nurseryman or county Extension agent.)

Shade trees are most effective when they are planted on the west side of your house. This will provide protection from afternoon sun, which generates the most intense heat of the day. Late-afternoon sun is less intense, but it is still hot. Since the sun is low, just above the horizon toward the northwest, small trees (even shrubs) in that area of your garden can intercept that last bit of summer heat. Evergreens can be used here, since this location will not affect the winter sun, which sets in the southwest.

Even the morning sun, especially in the Lower South, will put a strain on your home's cooling system. A shade tree or two on the east side of your home reduces that burden.

Large, unshaded expanses of paving, such as driveways, walks, and terraces, collect heat during the day and radiate it long after the sun goes down. Light-colored paving also reflects sunlight, which can cause an annoying glare and make it feel hotter than it actually is.

To shade paved areas, plant deciduous trees or shrubs on the west side of the area. If you are planning a paved terrace for a sunny spot, consider a wooden deck instead. Wood does not store or reflect heat like paving materials do.

VINES SHADE QUICKLY

Shade trees, of course, take time to grow. For more immediate results, consider fast-growing deciduous vines. Sweet autumn clematis, Japanese wisteria, and muscadine grape are all suitable; consult your local nurseryman or county Extension agent for others that are adapted to

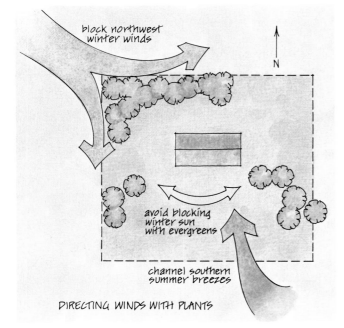

DIRECTING WINDS WITH PLANTS

your area. Not only can these vines be used to blanket walls and insulate them from the sun's heat, but you can plant them to grow over an arbor to shade a terrace, window, or wall. Like deciduous trees, they will thwart the summer sun but drop their leaves to admit the warmth of the winter sun.

COLOR AND SOUND HELP, TOO

While the shade of trees, shrubs, and vines can actually lower the temperature, color and sound in your garden can make it seem cooler than it actually is. The sound of water splashing from a fountain, for example, suggests a cooler environment even if the day is warm and humid.

Color has a similar effect. Orange, yellow, and red are associated with warmth, while white, blue, and green suggest coolness. To take advantage of these color-temperature associations, consider using more cool-colored plants in your garden: white and blue flowers and plants with light, clear green foliage.

BREAKING WINTER WINDS, USING SUMMER BREEZES

Your garden's contributions to energy savings do not drop off with the leaves in autumn. Evergreen trees and shrubs buffer chilling winter winds, reducing their strength and deflecting them away from your home. In windy regions like Texas, Oklahoma, and mountainous areas of the South, evergreen windbreaks can save homeowners as much as 30 percent on their heating bills.

When planted perpendicular to prevailing winter winds (usually from the north or northwest), evergreens are effective windbreaks for surprising distances. Their dense mass of needles deflects the wind over the trees and creates a dead-air pocket on the leeward side of the trees for a distance of 4 to 6 times their height. This

means that the trees do not have to be planted next to your house to greatly reduce severe wind blasts. An evergreen 10 feet tall will protect an area extending 40 to 60 feet downwind.

The effectiveness of the windbreak depends on its density, so use trees like spruce, fir, pine, hemlock, or cedar; stagger them in twin or triple rows spaced 10 to 15 feet apart. If tight on space, even a single row of a dense evergreen like Canadian hemlock is better than none at all.

Wind is appreciated at times, too. Evergreen and deciduous trees can channel summer breezes across your terrace and through your home. Summer breezes are usually from the south or southwest, so plant the trees in an angled row to deflect and channel the breezes through your outdoor living areas.

TIPS ON SHADE TREES

—Select shade trees that are native to your region of the South. Since natives prefer the climate and soil conditions indigenous to the area, they will be much easier to establish and may grow faster.

—Consider planting trees like those of your neighbor. By matching his trees, you make both gardens appear to be larger.

—Do not buy the largest trees you can find. Younger trees recover more quickly from the shock of planting; a 12-foot tree, for example, usually catches up to the size of a 20-foot specimen in three years. In addition, 8- to 10-foot trees are easier to handle, less expensive, and grow faster than larger ones.

—Plant trees during fall or winter. This lets the roots become well established during the dormant season, resulting in more vigorous top growth (the part that does the shading) in the spring and summer.

—Avoid planting trees too near power lines. Swaying trees in a strong wind may sever them. In these areas, you may need to use small trees or vines for shading.

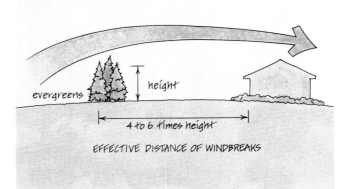

EFFECTIVE DISTANCE OF WINDBREAKS

Look Again, It's a Prime Site

For years, this "unbuildable" lot stood vacant in a choice subdivision. Now an architect's creative approach has turned the problems of the site into advantages.

The house perches on a hillside—but it is not a mountain home. Quarter-round decks are sheltered places to sit, and a glass bay puts the library end of the living room right in the trees. A creek babbles below bedroom windows.

It is in a subdivision. But as the architect says, "If ever a site dictated the design of a house, this is it." While its heavily wooded acre and a half were appealing, a 20-foot drop to a creek and a sewer easement made building on its very center—about one-third of the land—unfeasible. Building in front of the creek would have put the house too close to the street. The only place left was the back of the lot, behind the creek.

An innovative plan was able to turn those shortcomings into assets, however. The distance from the street and the wooded lot created privacy even for the rooms on the front and the library's glass bay. A deck off the master bedroom is also on the streetside, but hidden by trees. Still another larger deck off a lower-level playroom extends right up to the creek, an enviable setting for outdoor living.

Above, right: Entrance to the house is really at the "back," the side farthest from the street. But entering on this highest level avoids unnecessary steps inside. The children's bedrooms are downstairs, and a loft overlooks the living room.

Left and bottom right: The only area suitable for construction on this site was at the back of the lot, behind a creek. The architect designed a home that nestles into the hillside overlooking the stream. It is a house with lots of privacy, screened by the depth of the lot, which is heavily wooded.

The View Is Grand from Here

Good siting can do more than salvage an undesirable lot; it can enhance a premium location. Careful positioning of this house beautifully complements the contours of the land.

This relatively small Texas house (2500 square feet) is built on the highest hill in Nacogdoches County, Texas. The owners had come to the family farm every summer as children and maintained fond memories of the countryside. When time came to build a retirement home, they wanted to utilize this site.

The highest hill in the county was an enviable building site, but it was important to the couple that the house design complement the hill itself. As a result, the house was built on the slope of the hill, not quite at the top, but high enough for a spectacular view. Their architect pointed out that a house on the crest would flatten the hill, diminishing its natural beauty. The house serves, in a sense, as a staircase for the hill: It ascends on four different levels from the garage. The rooms are organized on a linear plan, so that in no spot is the house wider than the width of a single room. With operable sashes in the windows, this floor plan also provides excellent cross ventilation. During the colder months, the garage acts as a buffer to the north winds.

The summit of the hill nearly obscures their view of commercial development on the highway below. Yet the house is carefully positioned so that winter sun can still reach the porch and living areas, providing some passive solar aspects when needed.

Right: The family sitting and dining area juts out into the vast Texas landscape in one big bay. On the highest hill around, it makes a dramatic spot to watch thunderstorms in this big sky country.

Above: The house was thoughtfully sited on the slope of the hill after the architect pointed out that building on the crest would flatten the hill, destroying some of its natural beauty. Now they enjoy the best of both: an impressive view and the natural crest of the hill.

Left: A nighttime shot makes evident the variety of window shapes and sizes. The diversity is an architectural reference to older farmhouses of the area where a number of additions over the years has resulted in a house with many different windows.

Far left: The owners wanted to use as many elements as possible from typical East Texas farmhouses. Up close, the balustrade, scalloped columns, and shingles add a touch of Victorian charm, which softens the more contemporary form of the house.

Building with, not against, the Land

Land-sensitive developments can benefit homeowners in many ways: a more livable home, energy efficiency, and fewer problems with the site. Here are some standards to look for if you buy.

I t is not unusual for the developers of a new subdivision to wipe out the essential character of the countryside, bulldozing away all natural features. Fortunately, for the landscape and for the home buyer, more and more responsible developers now make a point of working with the land rather than against it.

A good master plan is sensitive to the topography of the property. One of the most successful plans is one in which streets generally ride the ridges with houses dropped down on either side. Most houses then will have daylight basements—full living areas with views to the woods—along with the main living space above. Also, the best natural features of the land are retained.

But important as the master plan is, what really distinguishes a good development is the follow-through. Look for developers who rely on deed restrictions to control tree removal, signage, and other aspects of building. You are usually assured of careful supervision when there is a staff landscape architect who reviews each site for such major considerations as how the house sits on the lot, where driveway and parking go, and whether any problems are created (such as drainage).

While each site is considered individually, there are two critical factors applied to every house that affect the total appearance of a well-planned neighborhood: Trees and land forms

Left: Trees and natural land contours should be preserved at the front of lots as well as to the sides and rear, so neighborhoods keep a wooded look. This natural mound gives privacy to a corner lot.

Above and right: These houses benefited from individual siting by a professional landscape architect, both for aesthetics and to anticipate drainage problems. Subtle colors in brick, paint, stain, and roof shingles help houses blend into the wooded setting. Side-entering garages and carefully routed driveways help keep cars out of view. A compact Williamsburg style is relatively easy to fit on sloping sites.

are kept intact, even those between the house and the street; and side-entering garages are used to keep the street frontage from being littered with cars.

For the best possible siting, the landscape architect should meet the builder on the site to stake out the house foundation and driveway. The clearance perimeter is flagged and major trees within the 10-foot limit around the house are also discussed, with an eye to saving whatever is feasible. The bulldozer is allowed to clear only the drive and the house site; it leaves by the drive. There is no random landscape damage. Even the underbrush is saved for later selective removal, a factor that helps keep trucks and other vehicles from overrunning the site and damaging trees.

Along with siting, house exteriors are also important to the neighborhood. The emphasis is on materials and colors rather than on any strict architectural style; compatibility, not sameness, is the goal. The concept is houses of harmonious quality that keep their individuality. Brick, siding, paint, stain, and roof shingles are all considered, with subtler tones the rule. The subtle colors mean that houses tend to blend into the woods. The most desirable effect is that of houses sitting in trees rather than lining a street.

Along with the definable neighborhood feel, the individual homeowner reaps other benefits from the building-with-the-land concept: Careful siting helps avoid many problems, such as

Above: An aerial view of a well-planned residential area shows streets working with the topography and the undisturbed trees around the house. The cooling effect will help reduce summer energy use. Careful siting "with the land" also helps avoid drainage problems and eliminates the expense of landscaping a bare lot.

drainage, that he otherwise might have inherited; preservation of native landscape eliminates the time and expense of landscaping a bare lot; and retention of natural tree cover near house walls and throughout the neighborhood helps keep houses cooler in summer. The owner will also enjoy that hard-to-define quality that comes with a well-sited house.

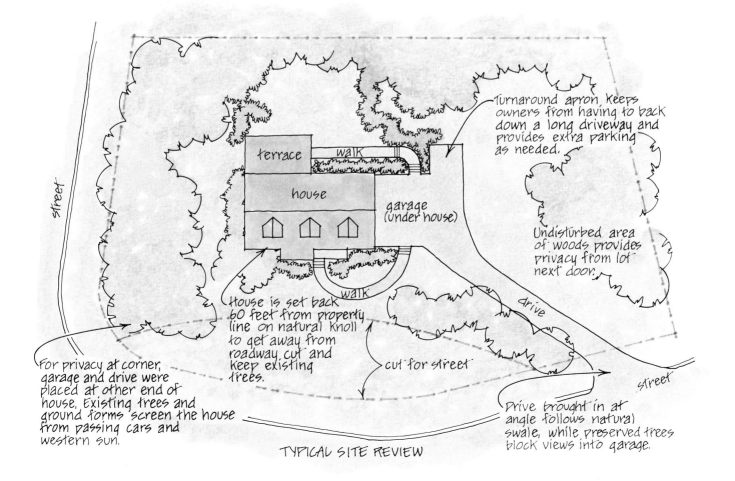

Turnaround apron keeps owners from having to back down a long driveway and provides extra parking as needed.

Undisturbed area of woods provides privacy from lot next door.

House is set back 60 feet from property line on natural knoll to get away from roadway cut and keep existing trees.

For privacy at corner, garage and drive were placed at other end of house. Existing trees and ground forms screen the house from passing cars and western sun.

cut for street

Drive brought in at angle follows natural swale, while preserved trees block views into garage.

TYPICAL SITE REVIEW

A Seaside House that Lives like an Inn

Tucked behind the protected dunes and trees of Kiawah Island, South Carolina, this house has its living area on the second floor for views and sea breezes. For the owners, it is a house on one floor—for their friends, a favorite place to visit.

The structure stands tall among salt-sculptured oaks just behind the dunes fronting the Atlantic, weathered but rather majestic—a little like an old inn. It is new, not old, and it is a house. But for friends who come to visit, the place might as well be a comfortable seaside inn, noted for good food and breezy relaxation.

The height of the house serves both practical and aesthetic purposes. To meet storm-tide requirements, the lower floor had to be above a specified elevation, so the whole house is supported on pilings above ground level. To take the full advantage of treetop views and vistas to the ocean, the main living area is on the second level. The top floor is actually a complete house for the owners, who planned it for an eventual full-time residence. For family and friends who visit, the lower floor works like a small hotel.

Left, above: Decks and a screened porch open the main living area on the second floor to treetops, breezes, and ocean views. The total impact of this treetop living is greater than the parts, due to the one-big-room effect, vaulted ceilings, the porch, and decks that draw you outdoors. The house has involved itself fully in the setting and style of living at Kiawah Island.

Right: The house exterior establishes its innlike character due to a formal plan executed in weathered, rough-sawn cypress siding. Massive 10- x 10-inch posts that support the porch and decks form a porte cochere, or covered drive, on the ocean side of the house.

Left: The porch serves as an open-air extension of the living room. If needed, ceiling fans stir a breeze. Another feature, the lattice pediment above the screened porch, punctuated with a circular opening, helps set a playful mood.

Below: One big room centered on a fireplace and open to the kitchen encourages carefree entertaining. Heart-pine, random-width floors extend throughout the living, dining, and kitchen spaces.

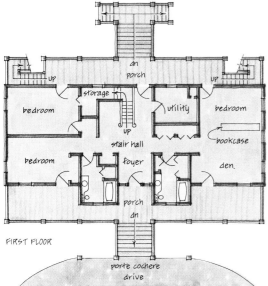

FIRST FLOOR

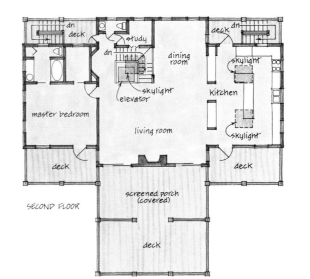

SECOND FLOOR

A Beach House for Three Generations

There is plenty of room for the whole family to spend time together—or be alone—at this Florida beach house. It is designed for years of enjoyment.

Originally, the owners of this Clearwater, Florida, beach home had planned to renovate an old, Spanish-style cottage by adding a second story. But when the cottage turned out to be in such bad condition that it was not worth saving, they tore it down and built the new beach house on the old foundation. Using that foundation meant the new house technically was a renovation, so they avoided the requirements that new houses be built on pilings to protect them from Gulf storms. They may have sacrificed some security to blend into a section of beach where most other houses are old and all sit on the ground. But they didn't sacrifice it all. The beach house has a steel frame under its traditional detailing.

Planned to be shared, the beach house has a distinctly different character on each level. Upstairs, the living spaces are more formal, with carpets and hardwood floors. Family and guests frequently retire to the upstairs living room for coffee and dessert after dinner.

The downstairs is more relaxed, with Mexican tile floors in the main living space, which opens directly to the porch and beach. Upstairs and down share some common elements, such as a wall of French doors leading to the porches across the front.

Throughout the house, windows have Key West shutters, which allow generous airflow through their oversized slats.

Above: The second-story porch puts people right in the tops of palm trees and provides a view of wide dunes and the Gulf.

Left: With the moon rising in the east, the house has a distinctly traditional and tropical flavor. Living areas both upstairs and down open to porches overlooking the Gulf of Mexico.

Above, top: At the top of the house, the large widow's walk has room not only for people but for sea gulls who flock for bread tossed in the wind.

Personal Style

Even within the regional style that has developed in the South, there is room for the home with a delightful individual character. In their broad appeal, the homes in this chapter stop short of being eccentric. They represent the best of all possible decorating styles—a personal one.

Designed with Light in Mind

Arkansas barns, two years spent in Switzerland, and a steeply sloping site in an older neighborhood all were the inspiration for this house in Little Rock. The inside reflects an artist's sensitivity to color and light.

I t's really pragmatic," says the architect/ owner of the house he shares with his wife. The barns of northwest Arkansas inspired the simple form and steep roof slope of the house. But inside, the delightful play of light, the subtle use of color, and the rich texture of pine reveal the influence of their two-year stay in Switzerland.

Walls throughout the house are gray green, with subtle variations in shade from one wall to the next. Even the ceilings are painted a light gray green. White is used sparingly—for emphasis. Color comes, too, from the oil-finished pine trim used throughout the house. Clear pine frames all the doors and windows and forms the bookshelves that line three walls of the living area. The European influence is most apparent in this rich use of a simple material.

The play of light inside the house is still another feature that distinguishes the house. The owner/designer explains, "You don't need uniform overall lighting. Instead, we tried to get light coming from several directions so that it is balanced, but with pools of light for interest." With light coming down the stairway from the bedroom skylight and windows spaced around the four sides of the house, there is always the feeling of being surrounded by light.

Left and above right: A turned-wood column supports the laminated beams that, in turn, carry the second-floor load. A skylight above the central stair core brings light into the center of the house, balancing the light from the windows. The living area steps down a foot to provide a 10-foot-high ceiling. The gray green of the carpet, walls, and ceiling forms a neutral envelope for the living area. A reading table in one corner of the living room is accessible to the shelves.

Above: Located between the kitchen and dining area, the wood stove provides supplemental heating for much of the house. A brass sheet with 1-inch airspace protects the wall from heat.

Above: In the dining area, shelves store and display dishes. Pine pieces over windows are splayed at an angle, reminiscent of window openings in thick masonry walls.

Right: The master bedroom extends the full length of the second level; louvered doors screen ample closet space tucked under the eaves. PVC plastic pipe, painted white, forms the frame of the canopy above the bed. A skylight over the stairwell brings light to both the bedroom and down into the living area below. A dormer at the side houses the bathroom.

It's Cozy Inside

A one-room log cabin with loft provides this North Carolina designer a special home. For her, it is a way of living.

Nestled among the trees outside of High Point, North Carolina, is a tiny log cabin, smartly decorated with pine antiques and framed pieces of old lace. Here, a successful interior designer lives at a pace set apart from her career pursuits in town.

"I owned a few acres outside of town when I saw a newspaper ad for four small log structures to be sold to the highest bidder. Most of the buildings were in poor repair, but there seemed to be enough salvageable materials for one nice cabin," she explains now.

Having no idea what anyone else might offer, she submitted a bid of $275. To her surprise, the seller notified her to come and get the logs and stones. The next highest bid had been $15.

She moved the structure most suited to her needs, replacing damaged pieces with logs from the other three structures. The cabin has one small main room, 15 x 17 feet, with a sleeping loft above. One end of the front porch was enclosed to accommodate a new shower bath.

The stone fireplace that rises to the ceiling is made from stones used in the foundation of one of the original structures. Additional heating is supplied by baseboard heaters around the perimeter of the main room.

The chinking is cement rather than the mud and clay that was used originally. Cement is more impervious to the elements and creates a solid bond.

Guessing the location of the kitchen is a little game the owner likes to play with first-time visitors. Since a few steps will take you all around the room, there are not many places for it to be located. When guests give up, she opens a lovely, tall, stripped pine wardrobe. Inside is a

Left above and right: Looking like a throwback to earlier frontier times, this log cabin belies the style and warmth within. The cabin offers interesting ideas for weekend or vacation houses, though this owner uses it as her permanent residence.

compact kitchen center, equipped with a two-burner stove, refrigerator, and small sink. The backboards of the wardrobe were removed and added to the sides of the piece to accommodate the depth of the cooling unit. Shelves above hold dishes, pots, and pans. Hooks on the inside of the wardrobe doors give additional hanging space.

Since space is at a premium, all furniture or decorating items must also serve a functional purpose. For example, baskets hanging near the "kitchen wardrobe" hold vegetables or other foodstuffs. A small, stripped pine dry sink nearby is storage for canned goods.

Getting a rather large brass bed into the loft took some engineering since access to the loft is by a very steep ladder. A pulley, attached to the central roof beam, allowed all loft furniture to be hoisted up and over the railing.

A standard-size skylight, the only other "modern" architectural feature besides indoor plumbing, allows ample daylight to penetrate what would otherwise be a very dark space. Also, to help lighten the walls, displays of white or light-colored items, such as old lace and quilts, add brightness to the sleeping area.

"The key to decorating a place like this is to keep the items you put in it to a minimum. A few great pieces and you have it," says the designer. The furniture is handsome and well chosen, not just leftovers such as are often used to furnish a rustic log cabin. The stripped pine is light and has a polished appearance that forms an interesting contrast. Other items, such as a leather wing chair, seem right at home.

Above, left: The sleeping loft is furnished with a shining brass bed and other antiques. A skylight keeps the loft from being dark, while bright white linens make the most of light.

Left: A grouping of antique lace, beautifully framed, forms a soft contrast to the roughness of logs and chinking behind. A dainty piece of lace on a swing-out curtain rod forms a translucent covering for the small window.

Above right and left: The stripped pine wardrobe next to the ladder has a surprise inside—a compact kitchen. The three-in-one kitchen center features a two-burner stove, refrigerator, and small sink.

Right: The interiors are simple but feature several pieces that are more refined than what is usually thought of as cabin furniture. Stripped pine antiques are used for storage, while a few fine pieces of artwork highlight the rough-textured walls.

Living Lazy
on the Gulf

Simple materials and good design borrowed from a bygone day make this year-round beach house distinctive. The look—and the life-style—is laid-back.

This is not a vacation house, although every day spent here must seem like a bit of a vacation for the owners. The house is lived in year-round; and a lot of what distinguishes their house is in the design. In fact, it is mandated by the building covenants of the development called Seaside. From the choice of roofing materials (two-wood shingles or galvanized metal) to the picket fences out front (each one has to be different), the covenants shape the houses, and the whole look—in fact, the whole spirit—of each place.

Far left: French doors in the master bedroom open onto the screened porch with a hammock. A second set of doors at the rear of the bedroom also opens for effective cross ventilation. The simplicity of white furnishings helps the owners to feel cooler, too.

Below: Recalling a turn-of-the-century vacation community, these new houses at Seaside, near Point Washington, Florida, sit close together on an unpaved street that runs to the beach. Metal or wooden roofs, lap siding, and picket fences are part of the design requirements in the community.

Above: A small loft at the other end of the main room provides studio space. White-painted, tongue-and-groove paneling on the walls and ceiling recalls the beaded boards used a century ago. A semicircular fanlight brings light high into the room.

The coastal climate, too, has strong influence on the houses at Seaside. As in this house, screened porches provide breezy, shady outdoor living areas and also help reduce the temperatures of the rest of the house. Plenty of windows and French doors, properly placed, insure natural ventilation that eliminates the need for mechanical cooling.

The interiors reflect the casual, relaxed style of living that is right for the beach. The central living area, used for living and dining, is a 15-x 30-foot room with a high ceiling. Furnishings, too, reflect the easy-going atmosphere. An old table and director's chairs centered in the room are used for all meals. Out on the porch, rocking chairs and a hammock invite you to stay awhile. White cotton curtains, hung on dowels, blow in the wind. Even the kitchen seems designed with a "shrimp-boiling" in mind.

Above: A wide screened porch wraps two sides of the house to provide plenty of comfortable outdoor living space. The floor is pressure-treated pine; the underside of the corrugated metal roof is visible between ceiling joists.

Right: Interiors reflect the casual life-style of this year-round beach house. Ceiling fans, screened porches, and gulf breezes eliminate the need for air conditioning. A wood-burning stove provides winter heat.

212

Locked in the Past, Opened up for Guests

Nestled in the woods high atop Signal Mountain, Tennessee, this log cabin reflects the simpler times of bygone days. It welcomes weekend guests frequently.

Stepping into this 154-year-old log cabin turns back the clock. Many ingredients of a past era are here: the rustic look of hand-hewn logs, a forest setting, and the smell of wildflowers. Except this cabin is conveniently located in the backyard.

"My family had always wanted a log cabin," says the new owner, remembering the day a farmer in North Alabama consented to sell her a two-story log cabin located on his back pasture. After the logs were numbered and tagged to aid in reconstruction, the house was dismantled in the late 1970s and moved to the present site.

Instead of rebuilding the house exactly like it was, this generation of owners devised a new floor plan: one huge room open to the ceiling, with a living area on one side, a kitchen on the other end, and a sleeping loft above.

Utilizing all of the original materials was a challenge. But the talents of skilled local craftsmen made construction somewhat of a history lesson itself. Everything was recycled, including some old poplar siding added to the original exterior sometime early in the twentieth century. The poplar was used in counter tops, steps, railings, and other utilitarian items.

Ordinarily, a cabin's interiors would benefit from the light of only a few windows. But here a vaulted paned window was added in one gabled end wall. The result—nearly an entire wall of glass—gives the cabin a contemporary, updated

Above: The cabin is situated only a few steps from the backdoor of the main house, but the wooded area makes it seem isolated.

Left: A multipaned window vaults to the top of one end of the cabin, bringing in spectacular views of the surrounding woods. The soaring window, which also brightens the cabin interiors, was made possible by removing the upper floor of the original two-story cabin.

Above, top: At the rear, an addition with many windows takes on a completely different look from the rest of the cabin. White wicker and pastels also lighten the room and blend nicely with the sweeping views of the woods.

Above: An old-fashioned footed tub seems to be in the middle of the outdoors, but simple canvas curtains can be pulled for extra privacy on the wooded lot.

Above: A fully equipped kitchen allows guests to make their own meals if they choose, and it is convenient for special parties in the cabin.

look. Light streams in, and there is also a spectacular view of surrounding woods.

About a year later, an addition with sunroom, bath, and storage area was built at the rear. Since the original logs had already been used, weathered boards were stained a rich gray for the exterior siding.

Though the cabin accommodates frequent weekend visitors, it is a place for special entertaining, too. For example, at Christmas an 18-foot tree fills the space in front of the large window and glows with homespun finery. Neighbors from all over the mountain are asked in to enjoy the sights of the decorated cabin. At other times of the year, simple bouquets of wildflowers and greenery dot the mainly earth-toned interiors with splashes of bright color.

Right: The original log cabin was two stories. After moving it to the present site, the new owners opened up the central room to the ceiling for a dramatic, airy effect.

Handcrafted with a Fine Touch

No house can be more individually expressive than one that is designed and built by the owners' own hands. This one in Point Clear, Alabama, is full of whimsy and delight.

Though books on handmade houses gave inspiration, the plan for this house evolved through the owners' sketches of exterior elevations. Once the couple established an outline of how the house would look on the outside, they needed only to arrange the interiors for space and storage.

Then the fun of gathering all the materials and crafting a house by hand began. A nearby older house that was damaged by Hurricane Frederick provided mellow, century-old lumber, which was used for both exterior siding and interior paneling. Except for the front door, about $63 total was spent for windows and other doors, all vintage and purchased from a local wrecking company. Openings were made to fit around all found items.

With a total of about 800 square feet, the house is divided into two main boxes—the larger one containing the public living spaces and the smaller, a bedroom. The two are connected by a sunny bath, complete with skylights and a wall of windows. The larger unit consists of a combination living/dining room with a loft for guest sleeping or storage. To one side is located a small kitchen.

While the interiors have a rough-hewn look with all wood left in its natural state, joints and corners are neatly fitted together with finesse. The husband is a builder/carpenter by profession, and could thus give attention to details so that there is an overall finished appearance despite the roughness of the materials used. It took the owners and one additional helper six months of continuous building to complete the project. There is no central heating or cooling in the house. Ceiling fans provide air circulation during the summer months. A potbellied stove gives warmth in the winter.

Above: This tiny house was designed by the owners and built completely by using salvaged materials. The larger unit on the left contains the living room, dining room, and kitchen, while the smaller unit on the right is a bedroom. A bath connects the two units. A deck that runs the length of the house is as much a part of the living spaces as the interiors.

Above, top: The front door, a towering 11 feet tall, was originally a pocket-parlor door. By removing the rollers and stripping the wood of paint (leaving a few flecks here and there for character), the owners use the door as a pacesetting entrance.

Left: Wood for kitchen cabinets is cypress that was once the exterior of an old house. The old bricks were bought as a pile from a local brickyard.

Above: An antique footed tub rests beside the sunny wall of windows overlooking the deck and a small pond beyond. The large secluded site provides privacy with a minimum of window treatments.

Right: The bedroom, approximately 14 x 14 feet, has a beamed ceiling; the fan is used for air circulation during the summer. Recycled shutters serve as doors to small closets located on either side of the bed.

Credits

At the time the photographs were taken, these were the owners.

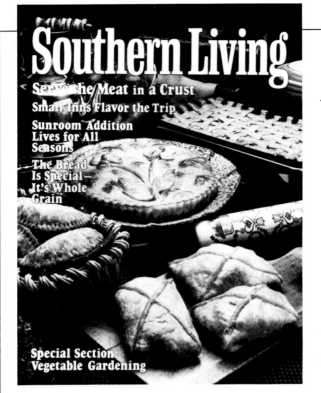